Complete Revision Guide

Brian Conroy
Trevor Gamson
Imelda Pilgrim
Marian Slee

Published by BBC Active, an imprint of Educational Publishers LLP, part of the Pearson Education Group
Edinburgh Gate, Harlow, Essex CN20 2JE, England

ISBN: 978-1-4066-1381-0

Printed in China GCC/01

The Publisher's policy is to use paper manufactured from sustainable forests.

First published 2002
This edition 2007

Contents

Writing

Exam questions and model answers

Acknowledgements

Every effort has been made to trace the copyright holders of material used in this book. If, however, any omissions have been made, we would be happy to rectify this at the earliest opportunity.
'Albert Docks' courtesy of The Mersey Partnership;'Easy Pickings' and 'Alarms' articles courtesy of *Which? Magazine*; 'How to vote' leaflet courtesy of Her Majesty's Stationery Office; 'Is it fair to put Mum in a home?' article courtesy of *Woman Magazine*; 'Meet Sundance' courtesy of the Whale and Dolphin Conservation Society; 'Ninja peril' and 'Fireworks: time for a total ban?' courtesy of *Manchester Evening News*; 'No time to draw breath?' courtesy of Macmillan Cancer Relief; 'North Cyprus' (advertisement) courtesy of North Cyprus Tourism Centre; 'Oxfam' (advertisement) reproduced by permission of Oxfam Publishing, 274 Banbury Road, Oxford, OX2 7DZ; 'Queen 71', 'Manchester United...', 'One judge...' and 'Hitting out' articles courtesy of Guardian Newspapers Ltd; 'Rhino adoption papers': we thank WWF-UK for permission to reproduce this text; 'RSPCA' (advertisement) courtesy of the RSPCA; 'Wheels are a wonder' courtesy of Mountain Bike UK; 'How green are you?' courtesy of *BBC Vegetarian Good Food Magazine;* 'Brit Awards Frequently Asked Questions' courtesy of BPI; James Villas web page by kind permission of James Villa Holidays; 'Morocco...', by kind permission of Voyages Jules Verne.

Introduction

About Bitesize

GCSE Bitesize is a revision service designed to help you achieve success at GCSE. There are books, television programmes and a website, each of which provides a separate resource designed to help you get the best results.

TV programmes are available on video through your school, or you can find out transmission times by calling 08700 100 222.

The website can be found at
http://www.bbc.co.uk/schools/gcsebitesize/

About this book

This book is your all-in-one revision companion for GCSE.
It gives you the three things you need for successful revision:

1 Every topic clearly organised and clearly explained
2 The most important facts and ideas highlighted for quick checking: in each topic and in the extra sections at the end of this book
3 All the practice you need: in the 'check' questions in the margins, in the practice sections at the end of each topic, and in the exam questions at the end of this book

Each topic is organised in the same way:

■ **The bare bones** – a summary of the main points, an introduction to the topic, and a good way to check what you know

■ **Key points** highlighted throughout

■ **Check questions** in the margin – have you understood this bit?

■ **Remember tips** in the margin – extra advice on this section of the topic

■ **Exam tips** in red – specific things to bear in mind for the exam

■ **Practice questions** at the end of each topic – a range of questions to check your understanding

The extra sections at the back of this book will help you to check your progress and be confident that you know your stuff.

Exam questions and model answers:

- A selection of exam questions with the model answers explained to help you get full marks

About this book *continued*

Check tests

- Use these tests to gain practice and experience in the key areas covered in this book

- Check your understanding of key concepts

Last-minute learner

- The most important facts in just two pages

Using this book

This BITESIZE book is divided into three main sections:

Poetry

This contains 19 units on poetry, in which you will consider the meaning and structure of poems and how the poets use language to help get their meaning across to the reader. Copies of all the poems referred to can be found in the AQA anthology.

Reading Non-fiction and Media texts

This contains a range of units concerned with reading non-fiction and media texts. In this section, you will see how writers use a range of devices to make their writing effective. You will examine the links between presentation and context and consider how writers target audience and purpose.

Writing

This section takes you through the different skills you need to develop in order to write effectively in your exam. It shows you how to focus on purpose and audience and presents, with examples, a range of effective techniques you can use.

There is a practice section at the end. It is a good idea to answer the questions as though you were in an exam. There are lots of reminders to help you work through the book – read them carefully and use the suggestions. You may find it useful to jot notes in the margins on some pages – this is your book! Look at the exam questions and model answers to help you structure your own answers and to give a clear idea of what is expected of you. Study them closely. There is also a glossary at the end of the book, which contains words that may be useful to you in your exam. Make sure you understand all of these.

Planning your revision

Students who get the best grades are those who plan their revision carefully, not those who try to cram it all in at the last minute!

■ Make sure you know the date and time of each of your English exams

■ Think about how much time – realistically – you can spend each day and each week on revision. Don't forget that it's not just English you have to revise!

■ You may decide to start revision around three months before the exam, in March. This gives you plenty of time to revise a unit at a time. Aim to work in 50-minute sessions with 10-minute intervals

■ Don't just revise something once – go back to it after an hour, then a day, then a week, if you can. This way, you'll become more familiar with the material and more confident

■ Draw up a revision timetable for the days and weeks leading up to the exams, for all your subjects – and stick to it!

■ When you sit down to work make sure that:
  - it's quiet
  - you've got everything you need in the room: pens, paper, books and a dictionary
  - you don't get distracted by the telephone or someone else's music
  - you have set yourself a time limit

Writing for GSCE English

During your GCSE English course, you will be asked to complete a number of writing tasks. These have been grouped into four main areas:

■ Writing to explore, imagine, entertain

■ Writing to inform, explain, describe

■ Writing to argue, persuade, advise

■ Writing to analyse, review, comment

Where you carry out each type of writing depends on the examination syllabus that you are following. Some types are tested in your coursework, others in different papers that you sit at examination time. Whatever type of writing you do, remember to plan and check your writing.

Planning your writing

This is **very** important. You need to:

■ gather and jot down a range of ideas that you could include in your writing

■ sequence them in the order in which you will write about them

■ decide on a paragraph structure

■ choose an effective opening and ending for your writing

Writing for GCSE English *continued*

Checking your work

As you are writing, stop at the end of each paragraph and read back over what you have written. Make sure your writing is still relevant to the question and correct any mistakes.

When you have finished writing, read back over the whole piece. At this stage, you may decide to add some words or cross something out. Check again for any mistakes in spelling or punctuation and correct these.

Whatever examination syllabus you are following, it is essential that you know what is distinctive about the type of writing you are going to tackle. BITESIZE English concentrates on writing to argue, persuade and advise. Check with your teacher which other types of writing you need to revise.

On the day

Make sure you know what day the exam is, what time it is and where it is. If you need to take books, such as an anthology, into the exam, make sure you have your copy. There's nothing worse than arriving late and in a fluster only to find you haven't got everything you need.

Get to the exam room in plenty of time. On your way there, go through some of the most important points you need to remember when you start your exam:

- Read the texts closely

- Read the questions carefully

- Highlight key words in the questions and key points in the texts

- Check how many marks are awarded to each question and use this as a guide for how much you should write

- Keep an eye on the time – it's important that you complete all the questions on the paper

You are now ready to start. We hope you enjoy working with BITESIZE English.

THE BARE
BONES

➤ Poets choose words that symbolise their culture.

➤ Poets use the way they speak to express their culture.

A   Poets often write about their own culture

1 They write about their background, where they come from.

2 They picture their way of life and show what is important about how they live.

3 Many write about a journey they have made from their own culture to a different way of living.

4 This journey is rarely easy and can produce a clash between cultures.

Remember
Remember to look for a clash between different cultures.

B   How to uncover the culture of a poem

Q What does the difficulty of the dance tell you about the poet's cultural journey?

1 First, examine the poem's **content**. In 'Limbo' a dancer has to pass under a stick without using his hands. To do this successfully the dancer combines foot and leg movements with great strength and balance.

Q Find two lines related to music. What do they tell you about the outcome of the journey?

2 Look for cultural meaning in **key words**. To do this, look first for words connected with limbo dancing. An obvious example is 'stick'. Notice how the stick of the dance becomes a means of punishment: '*stick is the whip*' (line 20).

The poet associates the dance with life on a slave ship. This links the limbo dance to dark memories of travelling from one culture in Africa to a different culture in the Caribbean.

3 The stick is also associated with the music which accompanies the limbo, the stick of the '*drummer (who) is calling me*' (line 37). Does the music convey a happier meaning? Or is it used for a different purpose?

Q How do the different meanings of 'limbo' add to the poem?

4 Look for words that have a symbolic meaning. As well as the name of the dance, 'limbo' can mean a place between one state and another. According to mediaeval Christian tradition, it is the name of the place where the dead go to wait before being sent to either Heaven or Hell.

Q What does the word 'dark' tell you about this cultural journey?

5 Notice how words are used to link different things. Here the word 'dark' is used to link the sea, on which the slave ship is travelling, with the earth on which the limbo is danced:

'*long dark deck and the water surrounding me*' (line 16)

and

'*the dark ground is under me*' (line 33).

C *The way we speak gives a listener clues about our own cultural origins*

KEY FACT

In 'Half-Caste' the poet uses two forms of language.

1 The language of his culture is a kind of West Indian dialect. It is related to Standard English but contains a rhythm all its own. It separates his speech from the more formal expression of westernised culture: '*wha yu mean / when yu say half-caste*' (lines 5–6).

2 The dialect belongs to a spoken tradition, whereas Standard English is associated with written language. Because these language forms have developed in different ways, they have come to represent different traditions. One result could be that speakers of dialect view the world differently from speakers using Standard English. This could indicate a feeling of alienation.

3 He uses some Standard English expressions – '*consequently when I dream*' (line 42) – as a contrast to the phrasing of his local dialect.

4 More often than not, he mixes the two forms: '*when yu say half-caste / yu mean tchaikovsky / sit down at dah piano / an mix black key / wid a white key / in a half-caste symphony*' (lines 25–30). Just as a half-caste child is the result of a mixed-race marriage, John Agard uses two types of expression and mixes them together.

5 He introduces the names of two people from westernised culture (Picasso, the artist and Tchaikovsky, the composer). These names may be used to emphasise his feeling of exclusion from western culture or to show that, despite his dialect, he is an educated man.

Q Can you think of any other reason for choosing this form of speech?

Q Why is the repetition of the word 'half' so important in the poem?

PRACTICE

1 From 'Limbo' select three key words that are used as symbols.
Show how each word is used through the poem to express various meanings.

2 In 'Half-Caste' the poet uses the word 'half' to create humour, for example, 'close half an eye/cast half a shadow'.
Does this mean he finds his position amusing, or is he angry with his situation? Find other examples from the poem where he uses the idea of 'half' to support your argument.

Analysing poems
'Love After Love' by Derek Walcott

THE BARE BONES

➤ Look first for surface meaning.

➤ By examining the language and structure of a poem you will be able to discover further meaning.

KEY FACT

There are five key stages to the analysis of a poem.

A First, find the surface meaning

Look at what the poem is about. Ask yourself: Does the poem tell a story? Does it link with anything in your personal experience? 'Love After Love' is about a meeting. It is an unusual meeting because it is between one person and himself or herself: '*You will greet yourself arriving*' (line 3). The meeting takes place in the doorway of the house or in a mirror. The person welcomes the other person into the house. There is an invitation to eat: '*Give wine. Give bread.*' (line 8)

B To discover the real meaning of a poem, look below the surface

Q Who do you think the poet means by 'another' in line 11?

To dig deeper into the meaning, look for **unusual ways** in which Walcott writes about the meeting. He says: '*You will love again the stranger who was yourself*' (line 7). Ask yourself, why '*again*'? Has something happened to this person's relationship with himself? Have 'they' fallen out with each other? Do you fall out with yourself? If so, over what? The poet says the person's other self was a stranger. In what sense can we become strangers to ourselves?

C The language a poet uses offers clues to the real meaning

Q Why do you think the notes are '*desperate*'?

- Look at the **types of words** that are used. The poet writes about the relationship between the two selves as though they had been lovers. He imagines them writing '*love-letters*' (line 12), exchanging '*photographs*' (line 13). They had written '*notes*' (line 13) to each other.

- The meal they enjoyed consisted of bread and wine. These are served at communion in church. By choosing words associated with religious love, Walcott is adding another level of meaning to their relationship. He puts their love on a higher, more spiritual level.

D The structure of a poem is a framework which carries the meaning to you

'Love After Love' is set out in verse form, though the structure is rather loose. The first two lines are of even length, but this soon changes. The uneven lines, the sudden stops – '*Eat.*' (line 6), '*Give wine.*' (line 8), '*Sit.*' (line 15) – create a sense of conversation. It strengthens the impression that Walcott is offering advice: '*The time will come*' (line 1). It is as though the writer has experienced this problem himself and is passing on something of what he has learnt.

Q What kinds of people offer advice to people in difficulty?

E Understanding inferential meaning is very important

This is the most difficult part of analysis. You are trying to understand what the poet is **suggesting** or **implying**. In this poem there are two chief ways in which the poet reveals further meaning.

1 One is the tone of voice the poet adopts. He gives advice with an air of certainty: '*The time will come*', '*You will love again*' (line 7), '*Give back your heart to itself.*' (lines 8-9). This approach provides a feeling of real hope. The difficulties can and will be resolved. The poet knows this will happen because he has seen it happen before. Moreover, the two selves will greet each other '*with elation*' (line 2).

2 Secondly, there are phrases where the poet has **compressed the meaning**. A typical example is: '*Peel your own images from the mirror*' (line 14). Think about what the poet has left out. Ask yourself what types of things you 'peel' off something. Then consider the word 'images'. When you look in a mirror, do you see more than one image? Is the poet suggesting a different type of mirror from the usual – a trick mirror? Or is he referring to the different images we have of ourselves? When you have asked these questions, try putting your answers into some sort of order. You may come up with something like:

When a person looks in the mirror he or she may see different images of himself/herself. They appear like stickers we put in books. The person is advised to peel away these images to find the real self in the mirror.

Q Explain what is meant by: *Feast on your life*.

Remember
This is not the only interpretation of this sentence. You may discover other inferences.

PRACTICE

1 The poem is structured on a series of instructions ('*Eat.*', '*Take down the love-letters from the bookshelf*'). How effective is this in conveying meaning?

2 Think about the title of the poem.
In what ways does the poem explain the idea of 'Love After Love'?

THE BARE BONES

➤ Refer to the text and develop your points.
➤ To do this, use the PQD formula.

A   How to find and use quotations

KEY FACT

When writing about poetry, it is important to support the points you make by referring to the text. Follow these stages:

1 Start with a point you wish to make (P).

2 Find a quotation that supports the point you wish to make (Q).

3 Try to develop the point you have just made (D).

KEY FACT

Set out your points and quotations clearly so that the examiner can follow your train of thought. Follow these stages:

1 Write down your point, followed by a colon (:).

2 Start a new paragraph.

3 'Put the quotation in inverted commas.'

4 On the next line, begin your discussion of the quotation.

Remember
Your examiner needs to see your use of quotation.

- Your layout should look like this:

> In 'Two Scavengers in a Truck' the poet is describing two old garbagemen in San Francisco as being out of place in a modern city (P):
> > 'and hunched-back
> > looking down like some
> > gargoyle Quasimodo'. (Q)
> The use of the simile here suggests that... (D)

KEY FACT

When using a short quotation, place it within the sentence.

You can use short quotations, of less than one line of poetry, to support your argument. Place the words within quotation marks. For example:

> When Ferlinghetti describes the garbagemen as 'grungy from their route', he creates a vivid picture of men who have been working long hours.

B   The essential elements

Look for the essential parts of the poet's imagery. Then think about what they mean to you.

For example, look at the following words related to different types of people and the ideas they suggest.

hunched	gargoyle	coifed	short skirt
bowed down, exhausted, crippled	carved face on cathedral, ugly, old, grimy	neat hairstyle, tidy, clean	modern, latest fashion, smart

Now consider these different types of people in the poem. How are they portrayed?

You could write something like this:

> The use of the simile about the gargoyle to describe the garbage collectors suggests that the men look out-of-date in this modern city, almost like ugly creatures carved on an old church.
>   The young people in the Mercedes seem in the latest fashion, fresh and clean.

C   Developing the argument

To develop your argument, you need a point directly related to the ones you have just made. You could contrast the two social types and write:

> The poet is comparing two old, dirty, unfashionable garbage collectors with clean-cut, trendy young people. (P)

This comparison is your new point. There are several suitable quotations:

> 'shoulder-length blond hair and sunglasses ... grey iron hair' (Q)

This will lead naturally to a conclusion:

> These contrasting types of people live in 'this democracy'. (D)

The conclusion should lead naturally to a new point

> But, although these groups of people live in 'this democracy', they are separated from each other (P) by 'that small gulf in the high seas'. (Q)

... and so on, linking one idea to another by creating arguments out of the quotations you have chosen.

Remember

You can refer to 'Two Scavengers in a Truck, Two Beautiful People in a Mercedes' simply as 'Two Scavengers' or 'Two Scavengers in a Truck' as we generally do in this book.

Q Find and write down two other quotations in 'Two Scavengers in a Truck' that show this contrast.

KEY FACT

PRACTICE

1   Show how in 'Two Scavengers in a Truck' the poet contrasts the lives of two different kinds of people. Use the PQD method in your answer.

2   Explain the possible reasons for the repetition of the following in the poem:
    looking down   *sunglasses*   *light* (as in *stoplight, red light*)

THE BARE BONES

➤ Remember the importance of structuring your answer when comparing two poems.

➤ Be aware of the type of language used in comparison.

From your reading of 'Not My Business' and 'Vultures' explain briefly the meaning of each poem and compare the ways in which each poet conveys that meaning.

How would you answer this question? Read on to find out.

A Meaning

KEY FACT

Remember This cannot be done in the exam.

1 Before entering the examination room, it is essential to have in your mind a clear understanding of what each poem means.

To be able to reel off a brief summary of any poem requires detailed study over a period of time.

KEY FACT

Remember Use the other chapter headings from this book as a checklist.

2 The meaning should be given in a brief statement.

There may be more than one meaning – for example, the surface meaning and a deeper meaning. Remember, in this part of your answer, do not include unnecessary description of the poems.

3 Meaning could include issues such as: identity, cultural significance, change, nature, war.

B Method

KEY FACT

1 Have in mind the **key methods** by which poets express their 'messages'.

- Verse structure
- Tone
- Use of imagery
- Sound and rhythm of the words

KEY FACT

2 Your comment on the methods used must always be related to meaning in the poem.

Do not make points in isolation: '*There is an example of metaphor in line 3.*' is useless. Always relate your point to its effect in the poem. For example: '*The metaphor in line 3 helps to emphasise the poet's feeling of loneliness.*'

C *Organising your answer*

When comparing two poems, deal with one aspect at a time and **apply your argument to both poems**. This is true whether dealing with meaning or method. Do not write separate answers on each poem. Read this sample answer:

Both poems deal with man's cruelty to man, leading to death. 'Not My Business' describes the effect of state victimisation, whereas in 'Vultures' the extermination is on a larger scale. In 'Vultures' there is also a comparison between nature and man. The vultures eat the dead because that is their instinct. The camp Commandant seems to be leading a double life to cover the fact that his trade is in death.

The structures of the two poems are different. 'Not My Business' contains three seven-line stanzas. Each of these deals with the disappearance of a single individual. The final stanza is, however, shorter, because the victim is denied the chance to 'savour' a yam. In contrast, 'Vultures' is divided into two main sections, to identify clearly two sets of creatures associated with death. Each section concludes with the poet's comment. The vultures' behaviour is shown to be 'strange' and the birds are portrayed with some humour: 'his smooth/bashed-in head, a pebble/on a stem.' The comment on the Commandant is more severe. The poet underlines his cruel nature in the phrase 'icy caverns'.

The poems also differ in their use of language. The account of the removal of citizens in 'Not My Business' is expressed in a matter-of-fact way: 'They picked Akanni up one morning'. The tone is that of a newspaper report, making the statements sound believable and also frightening because it could be your turn next. On the other hand, the language of the first section of 'Vultures' is more obviously poetic, for example, the use of 'harbinger'. The poet goes into gory detail to describe the vultures' eating habits: 'they picked/the eyes of a swollen/corpse.'

Other contrasts may be seen in the violence of the arrests in 'Not My Business': 'Beat him soft like clay'; whereas, in 'Vultures' the Commandant who controls a concentration camp is regarded as the dutiful father buying sweets for his children. His apparent innocence only increases the reader's sense of horror, because the 'fumes of/human roast' have already indicated the true nature of his job.

The poems vary in tone. 'Not My Business' moves from a tone of neutral reporting to the violence of each arrest. On the other hand, the shifts in 'Vultures' move from the poetic through the gory to the humour of the birds' domestic life. The shifts of tone in the Commandant section move between domestic life and the horrors of his work. The poet comments on his subjects: 'strange /indeed how...'. In 'Not My Business', however, Osundare allows the contrasting tones of neutral reportage and violent events to speak for themselves.

PRACTICE

Write a comparison of two poems of your choice. Remember to compare:

- what they are about
- the ways the writers use language
- the structures
- the tone and other relevant features.

The language of culture

'Unrelated Incidents' by Tom Leonard and 'Search For My Tongue' by Sujata Bhatt

THE BARE BONES

➤ The way we speak is part of our cultural identity.

➤ People who speak more than one language often feel most comfortable using their first language or mother tongue.

A Standard English and dialects

Q Choose any four lines of the poem. Re-write them in Standard English.

1 Before Standard English, everybody in Britain spoke the dialect of their area. Because political power came to be situated in the south-east of England, the accent of the educated people from this area became the accent of the establishment. This way of speaking came to be called received pronunciation (RP for short). Most national newsreaders speak in RP.

Q Try reading the poem aloud. You might find it amusing, but has it a serious side?

2 The speaker in 'Unrelated Incidents' talks with a strong Glaswegian accent. He seems to be mocking a newsreader who is speaking in RP: *'thi reason / a talk wia / BBC accent'* (lines 5–8). This creates a comic effect.

Q Do you think it makes a difference if a newsreader speaks with a regional accent? Why?

3 The speaker suggests that newsreaders don't speak with an accent because they wouldn't be believed or taken seriously: *'iz cos yi / widny wahnt / mi ti talk / aboot thi / trooth wia / voice lik / wanna yoo / scruff'* (lines 8–15). By doing this, the speaker shows how this attitude is insulting to the viewer who speaks with an accent. Notice he is serious about getting across the *'trooth'*.

4 The way he speaks is his way of expressing what he believes in. It also shows he belongs to a particular group in society. This type of speech serves to reveal the group's cultural identity. And by speaking in this way, he shapes his own identity as well.

Q List the names of comedy programmes where the humour is linked to mocking accents. Name any comics you know who speak in dialect or with an accent.

5 Dialects and accents are heard throughout society. Through them the speakers express their cultural identity. But they can have different effects on the listeners. Some reactions to accents and dialect speakers are hostile: 'I can't stand a person who speaks with a _____ accent' or 'I can't understand a word he's saying'. Some reactions are friendly: 'I love to hear someone with a _____ accent'.

6 In media entertainment, accents are often used for a comic purpose. The humorous effect relies on the reactions of the audience who represent a wide variety of cultural attitudes. For example, some listeners find RP amusing because it sounds 'posh'. Some think speakers with accents sound common, or inferior. Others enjoy listening to, and identifying with, comics with a regional accent.

B Culture and language

1 In 'Search For My Tongue' the sense of cultural difference is expressed through language.

- The poet presents her argument in Standard English: '*I ask you, what would you do?*' (line 3), but she is suffering a cultural predicament. She has lost her mother tongue. Only in a dream is she aware of her first language, her mother tongue, Gujarati.

- When Bhatt uses this language in the middle section of the poem, she spells the sounds phonetically in English. In this way the reader is able to experience what it feels like to listen to a foreign '*tongue*' as if for the first time. By placing the Gujarati in the centre of the poem she is, perhaps, showing the reader that it is central to her.

2 Bhatt uses the tongue as a symbol of cultural identity.

- She wonders what you would do with two tongues in your mouth, representing both her native language and the language of the country to which she has moved. This image of two tongues emphasises the conflict within her.

- She likens her native language to a plant that would: '*rot, rot and die in your mouth*' (lines 12–13).

- In lines 31–34, after the dream, Bhatt suggests the tongue has grown back as '*a stump of a shoot*'. She traces the different stages of her tongue's new growth through the metaphor of the plant that '*grows back*'.

- The conflict of the tongues is finally resolved as her mother tongue '*blossoms*' (line 38). This image of flowering shows her delight in the return of her mother tongue. She has rediscovered her cultural identity.

PRACTICE

1 In '*Unrelated Incidents*' what ideas about language do you think the poet is trying to get across?

2 In '*Search For My Tongue*' explain how Bhatt uses the image of the two tongues to explore how it feels to move from one cultural identity to another.

The significance of culture

'Night of the Scorpion' by Nissim Ezekiel and
'Two Scavengers in a Truck' by Lawrence Ferlinghetti

THE BARE BONES

➤ A poet may use reactions to signify important issues.

➤ A poet may use symbols to signify important issues.

A In 'Night of the Scorpion' there are several examples of things that have cultural significance

KEY FACT

Every culture has things that are particular to it. These may include things to do with language, history, music, clothes and religion. These aspects of a society will reveal the <u>significance</u> of a people's culture.

- This is a primitive culture. The people are peasants and their homes have '*mud-baked walls*'. There is no electricity as they carry candles and lanterns. Clearly there is no medical help they can call on and no hospital they can take the mother to.

- The peasants who flock to help the writer's mother show the attitudes of this society. They ask for the help of God to '*paralyse the Evil One*' (line 10). Their response is a traditional one. They repeat formal prayers: '*May he sit still*' (line 18); '*May your suffering decrease*' (line 21). They believe that the scorpion's sting somehow represents a sin which has to be purified: '*May the sins of your previous birth / be burned away tonight*' (lines 19-20). They even see the bite of the scorpion as a means of salvation for the mother: '*May the poison purify your flesh / of desire, and your spirit of ambition*' (lines 27–8).

- The husband is described as a '*sceptic*' and a '*rationalist*' (line 36). He lacks the traditional beliefs of his wife's comforters, yet he is shown trying '*every curse and blessing, / powder, mixture, herb and hybrid*' (lines 37–8). In desperation he turns to the traditional superstitions of his culture: he even pours paraffin on his wife's toe and puts a match to it in the hope of curing her!

- The poet shows his viewpoint in the way he presents the events. His irritation with the peasants is shown in his description of them. They are compared with '*swarms of flies*' (line 8). When they prayed they '*buzzed*' (line 9). He found their efforts to help exasperating: '*More candles, more lanterns, more neighbours*' (line 32). He seems to have little patience with the holy man who performs '*his rites*'.

- The mother's attitude is shown through her acceptance. She puts a brave face on her suffering. Although she is in severe pain – '*My mother twisted through and through, / groaning on a mat*' (lines 34–5) – her thoughts are for others: '*Thank God the scorpion picked on me /and spared my children*' (lines 47–8). The significance here is that this is a culture where suffering is accepted.

Q What is suggested by the use of the word '*perform*' in line 42?

Q Why do you think the mother's final statement is separated from the rest of the poem?

B In 'Two Scavengers in a Truck' the descriptions show two distinct cultural groups

- The first group is introduced '*At the stoplight*' (line 1). They appear distinctive in their '*red plastic blazers*' (line 4). At first glance they appear smart but in reality they are tired, '*grungy*' (line 17) and the older of the two is compared to ugly carvings on an ancient cathedral: '*gargoyle Quasimodo*' (line 22). The suggestion is that he has become deformed by the work and that, like the original Quasimodo lurking in Notre Dame, he should not be seen.

- A contrasting group is represented by the smart young things in the Mercedes. In contrast to the scavengers, they are fashionably dressed in '*a hip three-piece linen suit*' (line 11) and '*a short skirt and colored stockings*' (line 14). They are attractive and are described as a '*cool couple*' (line 28). They work in the clean, modern environment of an '*architect's office*' (line 15).

- The two groups are separated socially: '*as from a great distance*' (line 27). This is emphasised towards the end of the poem. Although they are held close together at the red light (line 31), it is only '*for an instant*'. They are, in fact, separated by a '*gulf / in the high seas / of this democracy*' (line 35). A democracy is supposed to allow everyone the chance of improving their position in society: '*as if anything at all were possible*' (line 33). But the poet has already signalled which group will come off better: the cool couple in the Mercedes. For them '*everything is always possible*' (line 30).

Q What does the poet suggest by describing the V ad as *odorless* (line 29)?

PRACTICE

1 Think about the significance of culture in 'Night of the Scorpion'. What do you learn about:
- the way the people live
- the things the people believe in?

2 Using detail from 'Two Scavengers in a Truck, Two Beautiful People in a Mercedes', explain how the poet makes you feel about:
- the garbagemen in the truck
- the cool couple in the Mercedes.

Symbols of culture

'Presents from my Aunts in Pakistan' by Moniza Alvi and
'Hurricane Hits England' by Grace Nichols

THE BARE BONES

➤ A poet can reveal something about a culture through the use of symbols.

➤ Symbols can take many different forms.

A Cultures may be represented through symbols associated with clothing

1 In 'Presents from my Aunts in Pakistan' different cultures are revealed through visual symbols.

Q How is colour used to show a contrast between the cultures?

- The clash of cultures is shown chiefly by comparing women's clothes and jewellery in eastern and western societies.

- The first stanza describes the vivid colours of female clothing in Pakistan. The salwar kameez are '*peacock-blue*' or they glisten like '*an orange split open*' (line 4). The slippers are '*gold and black*' and there is '*an apple-green sari*'. These colours are contrasted with the dullness of '*denim and corduroy*'(line 21), the clothing of females in the west.

- There is, however, a less attractive side. The bangles the speaker is given '*snapped, drew blood*' (line 8). This suggests that, although the poet finds her original culture attractive, there is pain associated with it.

KEY FACT

2 Symbols can be used to express alien features of a culture.

- The speaker says how she feels '*alien*' wearing the clothes she has been sent. This suggests two things: that they do not belong in her adopted country; that she does not have a right to wear them.

Q How does the speaker feel about her parents' camel-skin lamp?

- She expresses her preference for denim and corduroy. '*I longed for*' (line 20) shows the depth of her desire. Her preference for western fashion makes her original culture seem alien and foreign.

- The clothes were '*radiant in my wardrobe*' (line 37). This suggests that, although they may seem attractive ('*radiant*'), she keeps them hidden away.

KEY FACT

3 Symbols may be used to trace the history of cultural change.

Q How do each of the following imply a feeling of separation: 'wrapping them in tissue'; 'staring through fretwork'?

- Her clothes and the glasswork represent the time she first came to England.

- The words '*sailed*' and '*fifties photographs*' indicate how far back in time it was.

- The phrase '*Prickly heat*' (line 50) suggests the journey from one culture to another was an uncomfortable time. She was leaving a society of traditional customs. In Lahore women lived separately: '*screened from male visitors*' (line 62).

- Her mother's '*cherished*' jewellery was stolen from the car. This suggests that part of her past has been taken from her in this new country.

A

4 A poet's reaction to symbols can reveal a cultural position.

- Throughout the poem, the speaker expresses feelings of cultural uncertainty. This is often expressed in the way her clothes fit. Difficulties are hinted at early on with '*snapped*' (line 8) and '*broad and stiff*' (line 11). The clothes form a '*costume*' (line 22) which suggests they are not natural and normal.

- Nevertheless, her eastern clothes will not let her go: '*My costume clung to me*' (line 22). There is the suggestion that they make her look more attractive, more desirable – she was '*aflame*' (line 23).

B *Cultures may be represented through symbols of nature.*

1 In 'Hurricane Hits England' the poet appears to be forced into acceptance of cultural change by the forces of nature: '*It took a hurricane, to bring her closer / To the landscape*' (lines 1-2). The tension of the journey is seen as frightful. The force driving her possesses supernatural powers of great age: '*Like some dark ancestral spectre*' (line 6).

2 The poet feels compelled to address the powers of the hurricane. She addresses them by name: Oya, Shango and Hattie. She wonders why they are visiting England. The '*old tongues*' (line 16) of her culture back home in Guyana have reached her new home: '*In new places*' (line 18).

3 She questions the meanings of these symbols of upheaval: '*What is the meaning of trees / Falling as whales*' (lines 23-24). She seems confused, combining images of land with those of the sea. She seems to be lost at sea – '*why is my heart unchained?*' (line 27) – as though she is a spirit free to roam.

4 She allows herself to become a symbol of freedom by aligning herself with the elements of nature: '*I am riding the mystery of your storm*' (line 31). She herself becomes a part of this violent change: '*Shaking the foundations of the very trees within me*' (line 34). By doing this she comes to realise that '*the earth is the earth is the earth*' (line 36).

Q What different things do you think the poet is suggesting by repeating the word '*earth*' in the final line?

PRACTICE

Make your own version of this chart. Complete it by making notes on what you learn about how poets use symbols to show us things about cultural change.

Poem	The symbols used	What these symbols show us about cultural change
Presents from my Aunts in Pakistan		
Hurricane Hits England		

Interesting uses of language

'Island Man' by Grace Nichols and 'Blessing' by Imtiaz Dharker

THE BARE BONES

➤ Poets use word association to explore new meaning.

➤ Poets sometimes present scenes by appealing to the senses.

A A poet may write about different cultures by combining images in an original way

Q How does 'wombing' tell us more about the way the sea breaks?

1 In 'Island Man' Grace Nichols imagines the island man waking up near a beach with '*the sound of blue surf in his head*' (lines 3-4). So far it is a typical description of a West Indian morning. But the word '*wombing*' in line 5 makes the reader ask questions. Is the '*steady breaking*' of the waves wombing? Or does the '*wombing*' produce the '*wild seabirds*' of the following line?

Q Why do you think the sun is rising '*defiantly*'?

2 The poet imaginatively alters the natural order of things. The sun is seen to rise from the sea (like some gigantic creature of the deep): '*the sun surfacing defiantly*' (line 8).

KEY FACT

3 Nichols uses word association to present a new way of looking at things.

In the third stanza the man returns to sands '*of a grey metallic soar*'. Where the reader expects '*roar*' – grey metallic roar – the poet surprises the reader with a new idea: '*soar*'. Similarly, the poet uses word association in the final stanza. The waves are pictured as '*pillow waves*'. To the man in bed, the soft round pillows may call to mind the shape and feel of waves back home on his island.

KEY FACT

4 The effect of these techniques is to draw together two different cultures.

Look again at the first stanza. First impressions suggest an idyllic West Indian morning, but the island man could be living elsewhere and dreaming about what he used to experience. The sound of the surf could be '*in his head*' as a waking dream. There are more clues in the final stanza. Here island man '*heaves himself*' into '*Another London day*' (line 18-19). So the island man of the beginning and of the ending are one and the same person and, at present, he is living in England.

B Pictures of a culture may be presented through the different senses

1 The sound of words is an important feature of 'Blessing'.

- The coming of water is presented in the different sounds, starting with a '*drip*' (line 3), building up through '*splash*' (line 4) to '*crashes*' (line 9) and '*roar of tongues*' (line 11) as the people come pouring out of their huts and, finally, to the '*screaming*' (line 19) of the children. The poet has asked the reader to '*imagine*' it and then helped them to do so by describing the range of sounds.

2 Visual images complement the sounds of the water.

- Having got the reader to hear the rain, Dharker presents the glistening picture of the scene: the '*silver*' crashing to the ground, the range of utensils used to gather the water, the children's '*highlights polished to perfection*' in the '*flashing light*'. Dharker uses a similar device to that used by Nichols. She pictures '*the sun surfacing*'. Similarly, Dharker changes the nature of things when she writes: '*liquid sun*' (line 19). This combining of two senses (touch and sight) effectively presents a world of bright sunshine and rain. It frames the picture of the children excitedly playing. Notice that they are '*screaming*'. The poet has compressed different senses into one line, giving a dramatic impact.

3 Finally, the water is personified as it '*sings*'. Thus the poet has given the Blessing a human form, to match the '*roar of tongues*' coming out of the mouths of the people. The poet is referring to an event in the early days of Christianity, when people spoke in many 'tongues' or languages. This was taken to be a sign that God had sent down his spirit. The reference ('*roar of tongues*') gives a sacred and triumphant feel to the end of the poem.

4 But the conclusion introduces a darker note. The Blessing sings '*over their small bones*'. The poet brings the reader back to the real plight of the children.

Q The use of '*small*' may describe the size of the children. Can you think of another reason for using '*small*'?

1 Look carefully at the following phrases from 'Island Man'. Explain what they might suggest.

> *The steady breaking and wombing*
> *grey metallic soar*
> *to surge of wheels*
> *his crumpled pillow waves*

2 Read carefully the second stanza of 'Blessing'.

Explain, with close reference to this section of the poem, how the poet appeals to the senses of sight and hearing to create an effective picture.

THE BARE BONES
➤ Poets use imagery to widen the reader's understanding.
➤ Images may take the form of simile and metaphor.

A In 'Vultures' Chinua Achebe uses different forms of imagery to strengthen his argument

KEY FACT

Q What is the poet suggesting about the life of the Commandant?

1   The poem is structured on an extended simile.

• The glossary shows a simile to be a comparison using 'like' or 'as'. An extended simile is a comparison which is developed by the writer to explore the comparison in greater detail. In 'Vultures' the comparison word is 'Thus'. The poet is comparing the life of the vultures to that of a commandant of a concentration camp, where Jews were imprisoned and exterminated. He explores the lives of both the vultures and the Commandant at some length.

KEY FACT

2   The detail within the extended simile is often expressed literally.

• The male vulture is described as possessing a 'bashed-in' head (line 9). The poet is emphasising the physical peculiarity of the bird's appearance. This is strengthened by the disgusting physical detail of the vultures' habits: 'picked / the eyes of a swollen / corpse' (lines 13–15). This literal description serves to intensify the image; these strange 'pebble-headed' creatures are doing such disgusting things.

KEY FACT

3   The poet strengthens feeling by using metaphors.

Q What does the word 'rebelliously' suggest about the Commandant's attitude to what he is doing?

• The poet uses the phrase 'cold / telescopic eyes' (lines 20–1). The use of 'telescopic' enlarges our understanding of the birds. It conveys at least two ideas: the birds can see a long way, to spy out new corpses of animals; the word also suggests a science fiction creature with eyes at the end of stalks. The idea is emphasised by the following word: 'Strange'.

• The comparison between the birds eating carrion and the Nazi responsible for the gassing of Jews is emphasised by the metaphor 'human roast' (line 33). The poet is comparing a family Sunday dinner with the mass burning of human flesh. His description of fumes clinging to his nostrils is a quite literal one, but includes the word 'rebelliously' (line 34). Notice, though, that this is natural behaviour for the birds but unnatural behaviour for a human being.

A

Q Think about the different meanings of the word '*germ*'. Why is the word an effective metaphor?

- The man can be kind to some human beings – his children. This is emphasised in the metaphor of the '*glow-worm*' (line 44). The kind act is seen as a sort of '*glow-worm tenderness*', warm and shedding light into a world of darkness, hope amidst the suffering. The poet contrasts this with '*ice caverns of a cruel / heart*' (lines 46–47). Several things are suggested by this: the sheer extent of the Commandant's cruelty, the coldness of his feelings, and the darkness of the man's evil.

B In 'Search for My Tongue' the poet uses an extended comparison

- The comparison is based on two meanings of the word 'tongue'. One is the literal meaning of the tongue in your mouth. The other is based on the metaphor of 'tongue' to mean language. The poet imagines that she had two tongues in her mouth (two languages) but she has lost one of them (the original language of her homeland).

- Bhatt plays about with this idea. She wonders what would happen if she stopped speaking her original language. This tongue would die in her mouth. She imagines it like a living thing which dies and rots. She would have to spit it out. This metaphor is effective in stressing the physical unpleasantness of having to spit something nasty out of one's mouth.

- She presents the Gujarati in the centre of the poem, perhaps signifying its centrality to her life. It also helps to make the reader aware of the difficulties of dealing with a second language.

- When she comes across her mother tongue (Gujarati) in a dream, she imagines the tongue growing like '*a stump of a shoot*' (line 31). She describes its growth like the development of a plant or tree: '*the bud opens, the bud opens in my mouth*' (line 34). It even pushes aside the other tongue.

Q When the poet writes that the tongue '*blossoms*' what is she saying about the state of her new tongue?

PRACTICE

1 In 'Vultures' the vultures and the Commandant are each described as having two sides to their nature. What are these two sides? In what ways are the vultures shown as being better than the Commandant?

2 Explain how Bhatt uses the image of a plant to show how she feels about her mother tongue. Refer closely to the text in your answer.

THE BARE BONES

➤ It is important to recognise the effect of the environment on people's lives.

➤ An environment can be physical, spiritual, social or political.

A 'Blessing' by Imtiaz Dharker

KEY FACT

1   A person's environment can be religious.

In 'Blessing' the coming of rain is seen as God-given.

- The subject of the poem is water. The poet considers it both a necessity and something of value. She calls it a blessing, something that is God-given.
- The poem starts and ends with the effect water can have on the environment and the people. The poem shows how the people are physically made aware of the water's coming: '*drip*' and '*splash*' (lines 3 and 4). The flow has produced '*a roar of tongues*' (line 11) – it is seen as a gift from God.
- When the early Christians spoke in many tongues, it was seen as a sign that the Holy Spirit had descended on them. It had given the people inspiration, just as the coming of water gives hope to the people of the village.

KEY FACT

2   The environment can be seen as a physical one.

- These people live in poor homes on the edge of the city. Their housing is so insignificant that it is nowhere to be seen. The people appear only with the rush of water. They collect water in '*pots*' and '*plastic buckets*'.
- The people are not described as individuals. They are seen as categories: '*every man woman child*' (lines 12–13). Their individuality is lost in the '*congregation*' (line 12), a term often used to describe a gathering in church, and so the reader's attention is focused on the rain.

KEY FACT

3   The environment can be experienced through the language of the senses.

Q List the other types of noise suggested. How do they emphasise the people's needs?

- To convey the water shortage, the poet uses a simile: skin '*cracks like a pod*' (line 1). The effect of the drought is conveyed by the noise made in the silence. She describes the fall of rain: '*drip*' (line 3) '*splash, echo*' (line 4) as sound, not something we are aware of by touch.
- The noise in the mug is the '*voice of a kindly god*', which links up with the idea that the water is a blessing.
- The noise of the water is reflected in the sounds created elsewhere in the poem.

B 'Nothing's Changed' by Tatamkhulu Africa

EY FACT

1 The physical environment can affect the way we react.

- In stanza one, the environment is harsh: '*hard stones*' (line 1) – and neglected: '*weeds*' (line 8). But the weeds are '*amiable*' (friendly, easy to get on with), suggesting the narrator's feelings about the place. He feels at ease living there.

- Stanza two shows he has an instinctive feeling for the land: '*my feet know*' (line 11). His reactions produce a shift in tone: '*anger of my eyes*' (line 16). The poet directs the reader's attention to the object of his anger – a new, up-market inn.

EY FACT

2 The political environment can affect the way we react.

Q What do 'flaring', 'guard' and 'crushed' tell you about how the poet feels about the development?

- The poem is set in a country that used to operate an apartheid system, where Blacks were not allowed to mix with Whites. Although the system no longer exists, the poet says there is still discrimination. The inn is for Whites only, although '*No sign says it is*' (line 25). The Blacks eat '*down the road*' in the '*working man's café*' (lines 33–4).

- In the final stanza the man leaves a '*small mean O*' (line 43) on the window. He sees himself as a boy again, pressing his face against the new glass. His mouth leaves the shape of his lips on the glass. The '*O*' suggests his astonishment at the new development. He feels tiny against the sheer size of the construction. This leads to anger. He, the man, wants to destroy the complex: '*Hands burn / for a stone*' (lines 45–6).

Q What do the phrases 'I back from the glass' and 'shiver down the glass' tell you about the man's reaction to this new development?

- The separation of the cultural groups, Blacks and Whites, is presented through the symbol of glass. The phrase '*Brash with glass*' (line 17) suggests the new development does not fit in with the natural environment. It is garish and unfriendly. The Port Jackson trees, too, are out of place. Contrast this with the '*amiable weeds*' of the first stanza.

- The phrase '*I press my nose / to the clear panes*' (lines 27–8) indicates that the man has been excluded from the new building. The glass is a symbolic barrier. He can see what is happening on the other side, but he cannot gain entry.

PRACTICE

1 Look carefully at stanza two of 'Blessing'. The poet writes about physical objects (the municipal pipe and the utensils the children use to collect the water).

- How are these objects presented in the poem?

- What meaning do they bring to the poem?

2 Re-read 'Nothing's Changed'. The poem reveals the unfairness of this society.

- Select words or phrases which express this unfairness.

- Explain briefly how they show this unfairness.

People and places (2)
'Not my Business' by Niyi Osundare and 'This Room' by Imtiaz Dharker

THE BARE BONES
> A poet may present political threat by suggestion.
> A poet may question the effect a place has on a person.

A **'Not my Business' compares the menace of the state with the reaction of one of its citizens**

KEY FACT

Remember
The word 'clay' is usually a symbol of our humanity.

Q How does this description make the sacking sound frightening?

Q How does the repetition of 'waiting' in the final line sound threatening?

1 **The cruelty of authority is expressed in violent images.**

- The poet describes how one citizen, Akanni, was treated: they *'beat him soft like clay'* (line 2) and *'stuffed him down the belly / Of a waiting jeep'* (lines 3 and 4). The citizen is treated like a piece of meat. The image of violence is continued in the second stanza with *'booted'* and *'dragged'*. Notice how the enormity of the violence is emphasised by the *'whole house'* being *'Booted'* (line 9).

2 The poet presents the injustice of this type of treatment. He gives the reader the example of what happened to Chinwe. The injustice of her treatment is shown in the speed with which she was sacked: *'No query, no warning, no probe'* (line 17). The poet uses a group of three phrases with repetition of the word *'no'* to suggest she had no right of appeal. There is a sinister suggestion in the words *'just one neat sack'* for a worker with a *'stainless'* record' (line 18).

3 The reaction of the witness to this injustice is one of indifference: *'What business is it of mine?'* All he or she is concerned about is the comfort of eating: the image of the yam in his *'savouring mouth'* symbolises how the speaker chooses to ignore what is happening around him. This reaction to social injustice is emphasised in the repetitive chorus.

4 The poet then reveals the danger of personal indifference: it might be your turn next. The speaker finds his comfortable world destroyed. He is interrupted in eating his beloved yam. *'A knock on the door froze my hungry hand'* (line 24). He can no longer find comfort in food. Notice how the man refuses to believe this is happening to him. He is not hungry – it is his hand! Notice too that it is not the man who is bewildered by the intrusion, but his lawn!

B In 'This Room' the poet uses her room as a symbol of her environment

Before examining the poem, consider your own attitude to a room where you live. Ask yourself:

- Is it a place where you feel comfortable and safe?
- Is it a place where you can express yourself?
- Is it a place where you feel trapped with no escape?
- Is it a place that you need to re-organise in order to express yourself?

KEY FACT

1 **The poet presents her room through personification.**

She gives the room life-like qualities. So it is not the poet who is '*breaking out*' in the first line, but the room. This idea is continued through the first stanza. The room '*is cracking through / its own walls*' (lines 2 and 3). It is the room which is searching for freedom, a place to breathe '*empty air*' (line 5).

2 Dharker continues this approach in the second and third stanzas. Here the objects of the house are trying to break free, starting with the bed wanting to escape '*its nightmares*' (line 7). The bed is seen to be levitating out of its frightening dreams. The urge to escape is emphasised in the violence of the imagery: '*crash through clouds*' (line 9).

3 She creates a surreal picture of a crazy dance in the kitchen. She admits it's '*improbable*', but: '*Pots and pans bang together*' (line 14). The poet feels an air of '*celebration*' as they mark the stirring of '*the daily furniture of our lives*' (line 12). Her humdrum existence has been shaken up.

4 In the final stanza the poet shifts the focus onto herself. Through the agency of her house she has been released. She seems in a daze: '*wondering where / I've left my feet*' (lines 20–1). She finds herself outside rejoicing in her freedom: '*my hands are outside, clapping*' (line 22).

Q Why is it interesting for the environment to be seen controlling our actions?

PRACTICE

1 Do you think the speaker in 'Not my Business' deserved all he got?

To answer this question consider two things:

- the way the actions of the state are described
- the speaker's reactions.

2 Consider the following phrases from 'This Room'.

- *In search of space, light*
- The bed is lifting out of '*its nightmares*'
- *From dark corners, chairs / are rising*
- *The daily furniture of our lives / stirs*

What do these phrases tell you about the poet's reaction to her environment?

Sound and rhythm

THE BARE BONES

➤ The rhythm of the words helps to convey the meaning of a poem.

➤ The sounds of words can reflect the meaning of a poem.

A *The rhythm of the poem 'Limbo' reflects the rhythm of the limbo dance*

Remember to read the poem out loud to feel the rhythm.

KEY FACT

1 First listen to the rhythm. Note that some words or parts of words are emphasised. Those which are emphasised are called **stressed**; those which are not emphasised are termed **unstressed**. Mark each stressed syllable with a slash.

2
> You can see and hear regular patterns in the rhythm.

There are slower sections with stressed syllables reflecting a drum beat:

  /   /   /
   '*stick hit sound*'.

There are sections with a freer rhythm: '*night is the silence in front of me*'. Notice the regular 'falling' rhythm. 'Falling' means you start with a stressed beat and follow it with unstressed sounds.

> / / /   /   /
> *Long dark night is the silence in front of me*
> /
> *Limbo*
> / / /
> *Limbo like me*
> / / /
> *Stick hit sound*
>   /   /
> *And the ship like it ready*
> / / /
> *Stick hit sound*
>   /   /
> *And the dark still steady*

3 The rhythm of the words represents the drummer's rhythm, which creates the rhythm of the dance. In this way, you can experience the movements of the dancer, approaching the stick and gradually making progress under it. The foot movements may be suggested by the stressed syllables.

4 Towards the end the heavy beats become more insistent: '*up up up*' and '*hot slow step*'. You can feel the feet hitting the sand as the dancer inches forward. Finally the dance is over. This is shown in the slow, irregular rhythm of line 51:

> /   /
> *On the burning ground*

5 Remember that the dance calls to mind the suffering of the slave on board ship. There the stick was used to punish: '*stick is the whip / and the dark deck is slavery*' (lines 22–3). Notice how the rhythm of the punishment replicates the rhythm of the dance: '*knees spread wide / and the dark ground is under me*' (lines 32–3).

B In 'Island Man', too, the rhythm reflects the meaning of the words

0 Look at the irregular rhythm of lines 17–19. What does it suggest about how the man feels to be living in London?

1 There are examples of regular rhythm: '*groggily groggily*' (line 11) '*muffling muffling*' (line 16). The first helps to emphasise the fact that the man is in a dazed state; the second helps to convey blurred sound.

2 Generally the rhythm is irregular: The poet suggests a slow, uncertain start to his day. His head begins to clear when he feels the rhythm of the surf of his island back home in the Caribbean. This is shown in the regular beat of line 5.

/
Morning
/   /   /
And island man wakes up
/   /   /
To the sound of blue surf
/
In his head
/   /   /
*The steady breaki*ng and wombing

EY FACT

3
> Sounds of words are used to create the required atmosphere and feelings.

The poet uses alliteration to create the sound of the surf: '*sun surfacing*' (line 8). The sibilant (s sound) captures the noise made by the surf. She uses words which reflect indistinct sounds: '*muffling muffling / his crumpled pillow waves*' (lines 16–17) to suggest that morning cotton-wool feeling in the head.

EY FACT

4   The sounds of the words help to convey meaning.

It has been noted in the chapter on 'Interesting uses of language' (pages 22–3) that Grace Nichols delights in exploring possibilities of language. In 'Island Man' she expands the reader's understanding by introducing unexpected sounds. In line 5 surf is '*breaking*' – a usual description – but this is followed by '*wombing*'. The sound is soft and round like a wave. The wave is shown to be a bearer of life; it carries within it fish and hope for the community.

PRACTICE

1 Re-read lines 40 to 51 of the poem 'Limbo'. Show how the poet uses changes in the rhythm to build up to the climax of the dance.

2 Make your own version of this chart. Explain what the sounds of the words in the first column suggest about the Caribbean and / or London.

the steady breaking and wombing	
sun surfacing	
groggily groggily	
muffling muffling/his crumpled pillow waves	

THE BARE BONES

➤ Poets may search for personal identity in a social context.

➤ Poets may search for personal identity within themselves.

A 'Half-Caste' shows a man writing about his identity in a cultural context

1 The poet chooses as his subject a 'half-caste', a person with parents of different races. The poet presents the cultural position of the man. He lives in the Caribbean, speaks the dialect of the area and generally feels content to be where and who he is.

2 He explores the idea of 'half' in order to mock the idea of being categorised as a 'half-caste'. When he greets somebody he says: '*I offer yu half a hand*' (line 39). He even listens: '*wid de keen / half of mih ear*' (lines 33–4). He accuses his detractors of being blinded by prejudice: '*but yu must come back tomorrow / wid de whole of yu eye*' (lines 47–8).

3 The tone of his attack is savagely mocking. Remember that he does not feel inferior. In fact, he jokes about the European culture in his comments on weather: '*a half-caste weather*' (line 15). The poet shows how unpleasant it can be: '*in fact some o dem cloud / half-caste till dem overcast / so spiteful dem don't want de sun to pass*' (lines 19–21). His frustration with prejudiced people is revealed in the curse: '*ah rass*' (line 22).

4 He ridicules the term '*half-caste*' by applying it to symbols of western culture. He describes the music of Tchaikovsky as if somebody sat '*down at dah piano / an mix a black key / wid a white key / in a half-caste symphony*' (lines 27–30). To reduce a wonderful piece of music to a collection of black and white notes is nonsensical. As ridiculous as denying a man cultural status because he is a half-caste.

5 He concludes by showing it is important for others to learn about his culture. He has already shown his reader one half of himself. Now he wants to present the full picture: '*I will tell yu / de other half / of my story*' (lines 51–3). But he will only tell it if they have eyes to see!

Q What does the speaker of this poem have to say about prejudiced people?

B In 'Love After Love' the poet considers personal identity by examining different selves

1 How many selves go to make up you? Think about the different situations you find yourself in, with friends, teachers, parents, grandparents, brothers and sisters. Do you respond in different ways to various situations?

B

2 Think back over your life. Do you find any differences between the 'you' as a young child and the 'you' of today. As we say when shown an old photograph of ourselves: 'I didn't look like that!' Then we add, rather uncertainly: 'Did I?'

3 Now look at the poem. It reads as if a person were advising someone about personal identity. But the advice is puzzling: '*You will greet yourself arriving / At your front door*' (lines 3–4). The situation is unreal – you open the door and there you are waiting to come in! If we see this as a metaphor the meaning becomes clear. The person's two selves are seen to be separated. The poet uses a symbol of physical separation, a door.

4 When it is suggested that we see our other self in the mirror, the meaning is perhaps easier to understand because it is based on a common experience. The image in a mirror reflects how a person is feeling at a particular time. It will change from time to time and reveal a different part of ourselves. The image is not always appreciated by the viewer!

5 The poet suggests a way of reconciling the different parts of ourselves: sit down and enjoy a meal together. The meal is rather unusual: '*Give wine. Give bread.*' (line 8). This seems to refer to a church service of communion or mass.

6 Our previous self is seen as a stranger, but one who has always been interested in our present self: '*the stranger who has loved you*' (line 9). There is the suggestion that the present self has been unfaithful. It could refer to losing oneself in a relationship and the need to 'find yourself' again. The poet indicates this by the love letters on the bookshelf (line 12). It has been a passionate affair, too. Notice, the notes are '*desperate*' (line 13).

7 The final advice is to '*Feast on your life*' (line 15). On first reading, this is a puzzling statement. For clues to meaning, look back at the bread and wine of the meal. In the communion service the command is to feast on the body of Jesus. So the command in the poem may suggest that the meal of reconciliation has a religious feel to it. It is more than eating and drinking; it serves to bind our two selves together.

Remember

Think about some of those photographs of yourself that you don't like.

Q What does this suggest about the meal?

PRACTICE

1 In 'Half-Caste' Agard uses the term '*half*' in these phrases:
Half-caste-canvas
Half-caste-weather
Half-a-eye
Half-a-dream.
Show how these phrases reveal the prejudice of some people.

2 In 'Love After Love' the poet suggests that a person can meet his or her other self in various places:
a In a mirror
b In photographs
c At your own door
d In love-letters.
What would you expect a person to learn about his or her other self in each of these situations?

The importance of identity (2)
'What Were They Like?' by Denise Levertov and
'Nothing's Changed' by Tatamkhulu Afrika

THE BARE BONES

➤ Some poets write about identity in a national setting.

➤ Some poets write about identity in a political context.

A **'What Were They Like?' concerns itself with the identity of a whole nation**

1 The background to this poem is crucial to our understanding. The Vietnam War involved chiefly the USA and Vietnam. It was a vicious conflict, during which atrocities were committed against civilians. The Vietnam War is significant in that a superpower with superior military strength in planes and tanks failed to overcome the will of a largely rural people.

2 Although the poem concerns itself with the war, it concentrates on the culture of the Vietnamese. Through a simple question and answer format, the poet explores their:

- household objects: *'lanterns of stone'* (line 2)
- religious practices: *'ceremonies'* (line 3)
- habits: *'Were they inclined to quiet laughter?'* (line 5)
- personal ornaments: *'Did they use bone and ivory, / jade and silver, for ornament?'* (lines 6–7)
- literature: *'Had they an epic poem?'* (line 8)
- communication: *'Did they distinguish between speech and singing?'* (line 9).

3 Levertov draws a clear distinction between what the people were like before the war and how they had changed because of it. Their light hearts had been: *'turned to stone'* (line 10). There *'were no more buds'* (line 15) after the children had been killed. The bone ornaments had been *'charred'* by the war. The use of *'charred'* seems deliberate and refers to the Americans' use of napalm bombs which burnt everything in their path.

4 The poet stresses the beauty of the people's lives before the fighting: *'When peaceful clouds were reflected in the paddies / and the water buffalo stepped surely along terraces'* (lines 22–3). The way of speaking was seen to be as beautiful as a song. It is described poetically as: *'the flight of moths in moonlight'* (line 30). It emphasises the people's gentle nature. But there is no evidence of this beauty after the war: *'It is silent now'* (line 31).

Q What do you think the poet is suggesting by 'turned to stone'?

Q What does the word *'surely'* tell you about how the people felt about their society?

B 'Nothing's Changed' is also concerned with the destruction of an environment

1 The struggle is seen as one between an individual and the state. The individual is at first quite at home in his rural surroundings. He feels at one with them. Nature is seen to be an integral part of his existence: '*thrust / bearded seeds / into trouser cuffs*' (lines 3–5).

2 The state has parcelled up the land and given each section a number. In the man's case his natural surroundings have been categorised as '*District Six*' (line 9). Although '*No board says it is*' the man instinctively knows that it is so: '*my feet know*' (line 1). There are more intrusions into his life. The new development '*squats / in the grass and weeds*'. Again, there is no actual sign telling of this change; '*No sign says it is*' (line 25) but the man and the rest of the community '*know where we belong*' (line 26).

Q How does the word *squats* serve to emphasise the feeling of intrusion?

3 The man finds he is faced with contrasting worlds. There is the world of his childhood where he feels at home. This is symbolised by the working man's café, where he feels at ease. The other world is that created by the developers. It is a world of glass, which the poet describes as '*Brash*' (line 17). It is presented as a barrier: '*I press my nose / to the clear panes*' (lines 27–8). Consider these phrases taken from the description of the café:

- '*bunny chows*'
- '*plastic table top*'
- '*wipe your fingers on your jeans*'
- '*spit a little on the floor.*'

What do they tell you about the attraction of the place for the man?

4 The man feels driven to do something about this attack on his way of life. His thoughts turn to acts of terrorism: '*Hands burn / for a stone, a bomb*'. He wants '*to shiver down the glass*' (line 47). To preserve his identity he wants to stop this development, which is permitted by the state. Remember that the state represents a kind of apartheid system in which a group of people is socially excluded.

PRACTICE

1 Re-read the first section of 'What Were They Like?'.
What do you think the poet hoped to learn about the people from asking about the following:
- lanterns
- ceremonies
- ornament(s)
- epic poem?

2 From 'Nothing's Changed' find at least four phrases which express the man's feelings about what is happening to where he lives.

Change
'This Room' by Imtiaz Dharker and 'Hurricane Hits England' by Grace Nichols

THE BARE BONES

➤ Change can be brought about by influences within our environment.

➤ Change can be brought about by the forces of nature.

A 'This Room' shows a person trying to break free and bring about change

KEY FACT

1 To express her desire for freedom, the speaker transfers her wishes onto her room.

It is the room which is seen to be wanting its freedom: '*this room is breaking out / of itself*' (lines 1–2). The room becomes a living thing.

2 The desire for freedom is shown as a physical thing: '*cracking through / its own walls*' (lines 2–3). Notice how the room is shown to be an essential part of where we live. The walls act like a prison, because the room is seen to be '*cracking through / its own walls*'. The room is said to be '*searching for empty air*' (line 5).

Q What do you think the speaker means by '*empty air*'?

3 The desire for change is shown as potentially disturbing. The image of the bed '*lifting out of / its nightmares*' (lines 6–7) is used to show this. The desire has a murky origin in '*dark corners*'. It springs from quiet beginnings when it '*stirs*' (line 13).

Remember
Look for the way things happen.

4 The change is seen to be violent. The chairs rise up '*to crash through clouds*' (line 9). The distance the chairs travel emphasises the strength of the desire for change.

5 The violence of change turns into wild celebration when the pots and pans '*bang together*' (line 14) The vegetables and spices form an excited crowd to witness this exciting event: '*past the crowd of garlic, onions, spices*' (line 16).

Q What different things could be meant by '*No one is looking for the door*' (line 18)?

6 The speaker gets so carried away, she begins to wonder: where '*I've left my feet*' (line 21). Her hands appear to have detached themselves and have gone outside to applaud the event: '*my hands are outside, clapping*' (line 22).

B In 'Hurricane Hits England' the poet shows how change can come about through natural forces

The speaker's relationship with the hurricane takes many forms:

1 The speaker views the hurricane as an agent. It is the hurricane which brings '*her / closer to the landscape*' (lines 1–2).

2 The hurricane seems to have its origins in her past. It is described as '*ancestral*' (line 6). It assumes the appearance of a ghost: '*spectre*' (line 6). The wind is '*Fearful*' (line 7).

3 The wind is almost like a god. The poet speaks to several hurricanes by name: '*Talk to me Huracan*' (line 8). The last one she imagines taking her back home to the West Indies.

4 She seems surprised that the hurricane should visit England. She searches for the meaning of this. She makes unusual comparisons: the trees are seen to be '*falling as heavy as whales*' (line 24). There is a momentary glimpse of the truth: '*The blinding illumination*' (line 19) in the lightning. But it soon vanishes.

5 The poet finds the storm has released her. She feels at one with the hurricane: '*I am aligning myself to you*' (line 29). She is riding the storm.

6 The purpose of the storm is finally revealed. It is there to show her that she can feel at home in England. The hurricane is seen as '*breaking the frozen lake*' and '*shaking the foundations of the very trees*' in her. This imagery shows us how much she has been changed by the hurricane.

Q Why do you think she says the wind is also 'reassuring'?

Remember
Hurricanes are common in the Caribbean.

Q What does the word 'short-circuit' tell us about the hurricane and its effect on the poet?

PRACTICE

1 Re-read 'This Room'. Explain how the poet uses physical objects to show us that change can be:
- frightening
- violent
- exciting.

2 Consider these phrases taken from 'Hurricane Hits England'.
Write down their possible meanings in the right-hand column.

Words to explore	Possible meanings
dark ancestral spectre	
old tongues	
blinding illumination	
crusted roots	
the frozen lake	

THE BARE BONES

➤ War's horrors may be seen through the behaviour of man and animals.

➤ War's horrors may be seen in the changes it inflicts on society.

A 'Vultures' compares the birds' natural reactions to death with man's desire to cause death

The poet does this in several ways:

1 He creates an atmosphere of gloom and foreboding. A grey and drizzling dawn is described as '*despondent*' (line 2). Images of death and violence, '*bone of a dead tree*' (line 6), are combined with an almost cartoon-like image of a vulture with '*his smooth bashed-in head*' (line 9).

2 The natural function of vultures is to act as scavengers. This is described in horrific detail: '*they picked / the eyes of a swollen / corpse*' (lines 13–15). The reference to them eating the '*things in its bowel*' (line 17) adds to the reader's sense of disgust.

3 Nevertheless the birds are shown to have some finer feelings. They are seen almost as a human couple and he has his head '*inclined affectionately / to hers*' (lines 12–13). The poet sounds surprised that even in '*that charnel house*' they made a conscious decision to '*tidy it and coil up there*' (line 27). The poet questions how love can exist in such a place.

4 There is a suggestion of war. There is a corpse and a '*water-logged / trench*' (lines 15–16). These references foreshadow the second section of the poem.

Remember
A charnel house is a place of the dead.

Q What is the effect of showing the vultures in human terms?

B The Commandant of Belsen is seen in different terms

1 The reader first sees him going home to his children, stopping '*at the wayside sweet-shop*' (line 36). The '*tender offspring / waiting at home for Daddy's return*' (lines 38–40) create an air of normality, as though Daddy was coming home from the office, when in fact he is returning from a concentration camp.

2 His is a gruesome occupation. Unlike the vultures who eat dead flesh because that is their function in the food chain, he deals with death as a matter of choice. The fumes of the incinerators cling to his '*hairy nostrils*' (lines 34–5). His heart is seen to possess '*icy caverns*' (line 46). He is labelled an '*ogre*' (line 43). Even in the germ of love he has for his family there is '*lodged the perpetuity of evil*' (lines 50–51).

Q What is suggested by the poet's use of the word '*perpetuity*'?

B

3 In the final section the poet challenges the reader. He asks a moral question: Is it better to praise an evil man who has a bit of goodness in him – '*tiny glow-worm / tenderness*'? Or should we despair, because that little '*germ*' of goodness is fixed ('*lodged*') in endless ('*perpetuity of*') evil?

C   *In 'What Were They Like?' the poet expresses her feelings about the Vietnam War*

1 She contrasts life for the Vietnamese before the war with their life after the war. She does this first by concentrating on their domestic articles, personal ornaments, religion and literary output. They reflect a peaceful existence. '*Were they inclined to quiet laughter?*' (line 5) underlines an untroubled life.

2 The poet then reveals the intrusions of war. The peaceful beauty before the war is seen in terms of the destruction brought about by warfare. In line 22 a settled way of life is pictured in '*peaceful clouds were reflected in the paddie*'. The destruction of it is seen in '*When bombs smashed those mirrors*' (line 25). The details, '*burned mouth*' and '*all the bones were charred*' refer to the use of napalm. Napalm bombs would kill by burning everything over a vast area, including all the oxygen, so that many suffocated to death.

3 The pre- and post-war periods are subtly linked in the development of symbols. In the first section of the poem, key things are identified:

stone   bone   poem

These are then developed in the second section.

- In the first section the '*stone*' is associated with the calmness of evening; in the second '*stone*' has become a cruel symbol of change:

'*lanterns of stone*' become '*hearts turned to stone*'

4 The poet asks a very important question about their society. She wonders if it was celebrated in literature, if '*they had an epic poem?*' Epic poetry shows what a society holds valuable, as in Homer's '*Odyssey*'. The answer in section 5 is not clear. Perhaps stories about the nation were handed down by word of mouth: '*maybe fathers told their sons old tales*' (line 24).

NB: To learn more about the structure of this poem refer to the next chapter.

Q Why do the people no longer laugh or sing?

PRACTICE

1 Re-read 'Vultures'. In what ways are the vultures and the Commandant shown to be:

- similar
- different?

What is the poet trying to show the reader through this comparison?

2 In 'What Were They Like?' what does the reader learn about the damage done to the people and their culture by the war?

Structure

'Night of the Scorpion' by Nissim Ezekiel and
'What Were They Like?' by Denise Levertov

THE BARE BONES

➤ Structure gives shape to a poem.

➤ Structure is used to organise the ideas in a poem.

'Night of the Scorpion' appears to be one long piece of verse, with a three-line conclusion.

A   The structure contains a number of different features

1 The opening section is a statement of what happened to the poet's mother: '*I remember the night my mother / was stung by a scorpion*'. This sounds like a newspaper account. An eye-witness is telling the reader what happened.

2 Lines 2 to 7 introduce the scorpion, telling the reader how he came to be where he was: '*steady rain had driven him*' (line 3). He is presented as a victim of circumstance, not deliberately wanting to cause suffering. He stings the poet's mother and runs off.

3 The next section (lines 8–15) describes the arrival of the peasants with their lanterns, ironically '*throwing giant scorpion shadows*' on the walls. Their reaction highlights their belief in the scorpion's power. Their search for the scorpion is unsuccessful and they '*clicked their tongues*' disapprovingly.

4 The next section (lines 16 –28) contains the peasants' incantation. The lines are used to express prayer – the peasants are looking for divine help: '*May the sins*' (line 19), '*May your suffering decrease*' (line 21). They act as a chorus commenting on human suffering: '*May the sum of evil / balanced in this unreal world / against the sum of good*' (lines 23–5).

5 The focus shifts to the narrator, or reporter, for two lines (29–30). There follows a satirical passage which mocks the behaviour of the peasants: '*More candles, more lanterns*' (line 32).

6 The poet shows the contrast between the father's beliefs and his actual behaviour when put to the test (lines 36–43). A flat statement follows, to the effect that the scorpion had lost its sting.

7 The final three lines are isolated from the rest of the text to emphasise the mother's final comment on the incident. She is concerned only for others: '*spared my children*'.

B ***'Night of the Scorpion' is written in verse form, but the patterns vary from section to section***

- In one part there is deliberate poetic phrasing such as '*May the poison purify your flesh*' (line 27). Here the clear rhythmical pattern helps to emphasise the formal nature of the peasants' prayers.

- In other parts, the incident is described in a more matter-of-fact, conversational style. When describing the father's actions we are told '*he even poured a little paraffin*' (line 39).

C ***In 'What Were They Like?' Denise Levertov uses various structural devices***

1 The poem is structured as a leaflet. The title reads like a heading designed to attract the reader's attention. This is followed by numbered questions and answers. The numbers allow the reader to cross-reference points, to discover how the two sections are related. Thus the poem may be read by reading Point 3 in the first section followed by Point 3 in the second section. This is an unusual but effective way of structuring a poem. It helps the reader assimilate 'information'.

2 The poem takes the form of a request by an outsider to the Vietnamese people or a representative of them. These people reveal their nature in the courteous response to the questions, addressing the questioner as '*Sir*'.

3 The question and answer format is designed to convey clearly to the reader what the Vietnamese were like before the war. The questions range from inquiries about their ornaments to wondering about their religious rites and literary output. These questions are then answered.

4 The purpose of the answers is to contrast the peaceful beauty before the war with the effects of destruction. In line 22, a settled way of life is shown by '*peaceful clouds were reflected in the paddie*'. The destruction of war is described: '*When bombs smashed those mirrors*'. This structure strikes a balance between life before and life after the war and emphasises for the reader how much has changed.

Q Which question and answer did you find most effective? Give your reasons.

PRACTICE

1 Re-read 'Night of the Scorpion'. The poet seems to sympathise with some people in the poem and not with others.
Explain how the poet does this.

2 Re-read 'What Were They Like?'
Show how the poet compares the life of the people in peacetime with their life after the war.

Structure (2)

'Unrelated Incidents' by Tom Leonard and
'Presents from my Aunts in Pakistan' by Moniza Alvi

THE BARE BONES
- ➤ A poem's structure can help to create a picture of the speaker.
- ➤ A poem's structure can help to create a picture of society.

A 'Unrelated Incidents' copies the structure of a news bulletin in several ways

Remember
Read this poem aloud to increase your understanding.

1 Lines 1 to 3 form the typical opening to a newscast. The thick Scottish accent, however, makes it sound unlike part of a BBC broadcast.

2 The content of the poem is then broken up into various sections as in a normal news bulletin. But, where a typical news bulletin would cover topics such as world news, sport and politics, the contents of this broadcast are decided by the newsreader:

(Lines 5–15) – He launches into a defence of his accent.

(Lines 15–24) – He gives a reason for not speaking like his audience.

(Lines 24–30) – He discusses correct spelling and pronunciation.

(Lines 30–36) – He defends his way of talking.

(Lines 36–38) – He ends the '*bulletin*' in the usual way: '*this is / the six a clock / nyooz*'. He makes a final attack on his audience when he tells them to '*belt up*'.

Q Imagine a famous newsreader breaking off to tell the viewers what he or she really thinks. Write what he or she says.

3 The language is structured to resemble a newscast. The regular pattern of three-syllable lines ('*way ti spell*') might represent the newsreader referring to the auto-cue. The lines run on with no capital letters to give the conversational feel of an actual newscast. Notice how newsreaders today present the news as though they are expressing themselves naturally, as if talking to a friend. This gives the poem pace.

Q Write down a small section from the poem; then explain the comic effect.

4 But the newsreader is clearly angry. He takes it out on the listeners/viewers – '*yooz doant no / thi trooth*' (lines 32–3) – and signs off with '*belt up*'. Remember the underlying question of this particular broadcast: whether newsreaders should always speak RP or whether it is possible to have broadcasters speaking with a regional accent.

B 'Presents from my Aunts in Pakistan' is structured in a more formal way

1 The poem consists of clearly defined stanzas. Their length varies but their inner structure follows a pattern. Each stanza is a combination of long and short lines.

B

Q What else do you think the costumes represent?

- The longer lines often contain description, usually of costume, such as *'glistening like an orange split open'* (line 4) and *'The presents were radiant in my wardrobe'* (line 37). The magnificence of the dress represents a colourful culture.

- The shorter lines are often used for incisive comments. Some are reserved for the effect of wearing the clothing: *'snapped, drew blood'* (line 8). This short line is like a quick jab, a stabbing pain. It emphasises the wearer's feeling of discomfort.

- Some lines are short so as to focus attention on the writer's thoughts. The brief *'from Marks and Spencers'* (line 39) makes the reader think anew about cultural influences. Instead of reading about a girl from a traditional society living in the west who likes wearing western clothes, now we read that her aunts who still live in a traditional culture desire western clothing too.

Q Find three other examples of short lines and describe their effect.

- Short lines are also used to present telling detail such as *'playing with a tin boat'* (line 54). This isolated detail increases the sense of the speaker's loneliness.

- The poet's rhythm varies according to the length of the line. The longer lines tend to flow with a regular rhythm:

  / / / / /
  'glistening like an orange split open'

  This regular beat exaggerates the rich feel of the clothes.

  However, the shorter lines are slowed by an emphatic beat.

  /
  'I longed' (line 20)

  The use of the short, slow line sometimes helps to emphasise the poet's reactions to what she has described at length in previous lines.

  / / /
  'like stained glass' (line 33)

2 Although the poem is written in verse, the events in the poem read like an extract from someone's autobiography. It tells the story of a teenage girl living in England with flashbacks to memories of childhood days in Lahore. These are presented as short asides: *'half-English'* (line 25). In this aside, or quick comment, she reveals her cultural position.

3 The poet allows the reader a clear picture of things by the way she **accumulates details**. She presents short lists of phrases:
'screened from male visitors
... sorting presents
... wrapping them in tissue' (lines 62–4).

Then she leaves the reader to think about these phrases so as to build up a fuller picture of these aunts *'in shaded rooms'*.

Q Find similar lists of short phrases; then say why you think they are effective.

PRACTICE

1 In what ways is 'Unrelated Incidents':
- like a BBC newscast
- unlike a BBC newscast?

2 How does the poet use varied line lengths in 'Presents from my Aunts in Pakistan'? How effective do you find this use?

44

Understanding issues
'Not My Business' by Niyi Osundare and
'Nothing's Changed' by Tatamkhulu Afrika

THE BARE BONES

➤ Look for the ways in which poets suggest issues.
➤ Poets often suggest issues indirectly.

Re-read the chapter 'People and places' (pages 26–7) to understand the relationship between people and their environment.

A The use of subtlety in 'Not My Business'

In 'Not My Business' the poet writes about people living in a country run by an authoritarian regime. The means of control are through the secret police. Niyi Osundare does not state what the issues are for the people in this society. Instead he gets his message across in quite subtle ways.

Q What does the word 'savouring' tell you about the man's indifference to society?

Remember
Look at the wider picture.

1 He focuses on the persona's attitude to the sudden arrests. The attitude is suggested in the eating of a yam. The man's only concern is that the police do not deny him this simple pleasure. In other words, the man has only a limited interest in what is going on around him. He does not concern himself with important matters, like justice, social equality and freedom. Perhaps this man is representative of mankind. Do we behave as he does?

2 The arrival of the arresting officers is presented impersonally: '*They picked*' (line 1) '*They came*' (line 8). The poet does not put names and faces to these people. Not knowing who is making the arrests can have a number of different effects:

- It can make a person more frightened.
- The word '*they*' makes news of an arrest sound like a rumour and you do not always know whether to believe rumours.
- It makes the enemy seem invisible as though '*they*' can never be recognised.

Which of the above impressions do you think the poet intends to give the reader? Give reasons for your choice(s).

In the final stanza there is no mention of the arresting officers. Only the jeep is seen. The reader does not even know if the man is arrested, because the poem ends with the jeep '*Waiting, waiting in its usual silence*' (line 26). The word '*usual*' makes it seem like a common occurrence. The reader can only imagine what happens next.

Remember
Action often represents attitudes and feelings.

3 The intrusion of the state into the daily lives of the people is seen to be violent. The indifference of the man to social and political issues is shaken by the violence of state repression: '*Booted the whole house*' (line 9). Notice how they didn't boot an individual but a whole building or family unit. The poem is not only about the state versus the individual but the state versus the people. The terror of the violence is summed up in the dramatic '*A knock on the door froze my hungry hand*' (line 24).

B 'Nothing's Changed' presents issues in many subtle ways

1 Although the title is 'Nothing's Changed', the poem is concerned with social change. The change is being foisted on the people. The people who come from a rural community are faced by powerful authorities which are taking over land in order to erect new developments. The people have lived on the land so long that they have an instinctive feel for it: the '*weeds*' are '*amiable*' (line 8) and '*my feet know*' (line 11). The developers are presented as unfeeling intruders, the name of the development '*flaring like a flag*' (line 18). Some of the land has been taken away and the local people can no longer gain access to it. There is a '*guard at the gatepost*' (line 23).

2 The different wishes of the people and the developers are represented in the symbol of glass. The new development is largely built of glass. This works in two ways: it is transparent – '*the clear panes*' (line 28) – and it acts as a barrier: '*I back from the glass*' (line 41). So the developers would like the people to see what the benefits would be for them, but the glass prevents certain sections of the populace from entering. Remember under the apartheid system the state was quite ruthless in its segregation of a country. There were restrictions placed on people as to where they were allowed to live. Blacks were forced to live in townships great distances from their place of work. This poem considers a time when apartheid has been abolished. The poet reveals a more subtle type of apartheid. People now are excluded from areas by reasons of money and status. It is still apartheid, but under a different name.

3 Those who are denied the privileges of the few feel resentful. The reaction of the speaker to this new development is one of revolution. He feels the desire to '*stone*' and '*bomb*' the buildings, '*to shiver down the glass*' (line 47).

4 The conclusion is an ambiguous statement: '*Nothing's changed*'. This could mean the revolution he longed for has not taken place or this is what it's always like in his country – nothing's changed.

Remember
We greet even small changes in our lives with suspicion.

Q What does the word '*shiver*' tell you about what would happen to the glass and about how he feels?

PRACTICE

1 Re-read 'Not My Business'. Write a letter to the yam-eater, advising him of the necessity of people playing a part in society.

2 In 'Nothing's Changed' the poet shows that prejudice can be hidden as well as out in the open. How does the poet reveal this idea to the reader?

THE BARE BONES

➤ Non-fiction and media texts are not poems, stories, novels or plays.
➤ They include newspapers, magazine articles, information leaflets, advertisements, biographies and autobiographies, letters and diaries, travel writing and reference books and ICT-based information.
➤ They are written to inform, to persuade, to give advice or to describe.

A What skills do I need?

You are expected to:

1 extract information from texts and develop your interpretation of them

2 distinguish between fact and opinion

3 follow and explain the writer's arguments

4 select material according to purpose and make cross-references

5 write about the way in which the information is presented

6 consider how effectively the information is presented

B Reading in the exam

KEY FACT

To do well in exams, you need to be a very efficient reader.

Follow these steps:

1 Start by reading the questions or tasks set, so you know what you're looking for when you read the text.

2 Then read the text once, so you have a general idea of what it contains. Don't worry if you do not understand or remember everything the first time you read it.

3 The **second** time you read the text, you'll be reading it to **look for a particular piece of information** needed to answer a question. This is known as **scanning.**

KEY FACT

You'll find it helpful to underline or highlight the relevant parts of a text to help you answer an exam question.

Refer to the text frequently to support your answers. You must give as much evidence of your reading as you can.

c Becoming familiar with non-fiction texts

- Non-fiction and media texts are all around us in the form of adverts, leaflets, information sheets, newpapers, junk mail, web pages and many more items.

- Get familiar with this type of text by reading some of the non-fiction texts that you see around you. Try to work out what techniques their writers have used to get their information across in an interesting and appealing way.

PRACTICE

Study these texts and work out why they were written and in what sort of publication they would appear.

A

How to Vote

This leaflet tells you how you can still vote even if you are unable to go to your polling station on election day. Providing there is a good reason why you cannot vote in person, you can apply to vote by post or proxy.

(A proxy is someone who votes on your behalf.)

For example:
- if you will be away on holiday (in the UK or abroad)
- if your work takes you away from home
- if you are ill or in hospital.

Some people qualify to vote by post or proxy for a longer period of time, not just at one particular election.

B

Castle: a large fortified building. The name comes form the Latin word *castellum,* which means a small fortified place. Castles were built to keep out invaders. Throughout history, castles have undergone many changes to adapt to changes in weapons and defence techniques. Castles in the middle ages were built on mounds of earth surrounded by a wooden fence. This was known as a motte-and-bailey castle. This type of castle was later built in stone. The White Tower of London is one of the simplest stone castles, known as a keep or donjon. Later, stone castles became more sophisticated in design. Castles such as Caernafon Castle in Wales have battlemented towers and outer walls known as curtain walls.

C

YOUR HEALTH

with Dr Kay Hadley

How can I heal all my burns?

Q I cook a lot and am prone to small burns on my hands and wrists. Is there any way that I can soothe these naturally and, perhaps, get them to heal more quickly? *J. Smith, London.*

A The most important thing after you have burnt yourself is to run cold water over the burn. This takes much of the heat out of it and helps to limit its severity. For maximum benefit, keep the burn under cold running water for several minutes and apply ice, too.

While minor burns can be treated at home, large or severe injuries should be looked at by a doctor, just in case you need medical treatment.

Pure essential oil of lavender can be soothing. Apply it several times a day while the burn is healing. This will help it heal quickly with the minimum scarring.

Extracting and collating information

THE BARE BONES

➤ To extract information quickly and efficiently, use reading techniques known as <u>skimming</u> and <u>scanning</u>.

➤ <u>Skimming</u> a text means reading it quickly to get the main points.

➤ <u>Scanning</u> a text means reading a text to look out for particular details or information.

A Extracting information

Remember
- Skim
- Scan
- Highlight
- Write answer

1 Skim read the questions first, so you know what you are looking for. If you do this, you will get an idea of the main points of the text before you even read it.

2 Skim read the whole text once to work out what it is about and what the main points are. Don't worry if you don't remember details from the text at this stage.

3 When you are ready to answer the questions, underline the key words in each one.

For example:
Name <u>four</u> ways in which <u>students</u> are helped to find <u>part-time jobs</u>.

4 Now scan the text, looking out for the information you have highlighted in the question. Ignore the rest of the text and only concentrate on looking for what you need to answer a particular question.

5 When you have found the information, underline it on the text.

6 Use this information to answer the question.

7 Write a focused answer – do not copy out whole chunks of text.

B Collating information

> **KEY FACT**

Exam questions often ask you to combine information that you have extracted from different texts. This is known as <u>collating</u> information.

- When you are collating information, you use the same **skimming and scanning techniques** that you used for extracting information.

- Use a **highlighter** to underline points on **both** texts. If you do this, you will be able to check that you have included information from both texts.

B

Using
information
from both texts,
name four ways
in which the
RSPCA helps
animals.

Remember

Make sure you:
- include the exact number of points that the question asks for.
- Use information from both texts.

Just £8 makes the difference between life and death

- £8 goes towards first aid and essential medication given to a rescued animal.
- £8 will help the RSPCA build and run animal shelters where abandoned animals find safety; where the beaten and tortured receive veterinary care; and where the neglected and ignored find love.
- £8 helps to pay the cost of starting a new RSPCA inspector's training.

WILD REFUGE

The more we encroach on nature, the more work we create for wildlife sanctuaries. Chris Hulme reports.

We Britons are proud of our reputation as animal lovers. In every town and city, there are countless people concerned about the welfare of creatures great and small. Unfortunately, that's not the whole story. The reality of life in any industrial country is that wildlife usually comes off second best in encounters with humans. Cars, pollution, building projects and downright cruelty all regularly claim casualties.

The RSPCA is doing what it can to redress the balance. The society has three specialist wildlife hospitals which treat injured or orphaned animals, always with the objective of returning them to their natural habitat.

C *Putting information into your own words*

KEY FACT

Sometimes exam questions ask you to extract information and then put it into your own words. This is known as using the technique of <u>reorganisation</u>.

- To reorganise information, follow the steps as in Section A. Highlight the key point in the question, and then scan the text to find the appropriate information.
- Use the highlighted information to help you write your answer, **don't copy it.**

PRACTICE

You will risk losing marks if you do not use your own words.

Read the two texts below. **Explain, in your own words,** the dangers that face some animals. Refer to both texts in your answer.

Adopt a dolphin

Meet Sundance. He pursues a life of fun, friendship and freedom off the coast of the Moray Firth in Scotland. A lifestyle which may not be sustainable for much longer. Pollution, over-fishing, capture and drowning in fishing nets are daily threats to dolphins like Sundance.

ADOPT A RHINO

Kinyanju is a black rhino. Not so long ago – only as far back as the seventies – he would have been one of 6000 in Africa. Now a monstrous trade has decimated these numbers. A staggering 95% of black rhinos have been cold-bloodedly butchered for their horns.

Today, Kinyanju is one of only 434 of these magnificent beasts left alive in Kenya.

THE BARE BONES
➤ <u>Facts</u> can be proved.
➤ <u>Opinions</u> are statements of belief.

A How to spot facts and opinions

KEY FACT ▷ **Facts can be proved to be true.**

Remember
Facts often contain numbers.

For example:
- In AD 79, the volcano Mount Vesuvius erupted.
  This figure could be **checked** *in history books.*
- Some of the world's highest volcanoes are in the Andes in South America.
  This fact could be **checked** *in geography books.*

KEY FACT ▷ **Opinions are what people <u>believe</u> or <u>think</u> – they are personal.**

For example:
Dogs are man's best friend. This is an opinion: it cannot be proved to be true.

B Telling the difference

Remember
Estimates are not facts. For example, 'It is estimated that 360 people are sleeping rough...' is not a fact.

Sometimes it is not easy to tell the difference between facts and opinions.

This is a fact that could be proved by visiting or telephoning the shop.

The use of the number might make you think this is a fact. But not everyone would consider the offers to be fantastic. This is an opinion.

UP TO **£100** free frozen food on selected models!

5 FANTASTIC OFFERS!

C Looking at the language of opinions

Advertisers often use language emotively to appeal to the feelings or emotions of readers. Language used emotively is a good clue to look for when you are trying to spot opinions.

Q Look at this extract and find two examples of words and phrases that are used emotively.

Easy pickings on the street

As a part of our car tests we check the security of doors, windows, boot or tailgate, bonnet, glovebox, steering-column lock, petrol-filler lock and sunroof.

Here we tell you what we've found. It adds up to a sorry picture for car owners and a disgraceful one for car-makers.

C

Another way to spot an opinion is to look for the words that introduce it.

These words are often used to introduce an opinion:

seem	suggest	may	might	should	could	would

These words all suggest **possibilities** rather than something that is definite and can be proved like a fact.

Look out for these words as you pick out the **opinions** from this extract:

> Buying a car is, for many people, the second most costly purchase they make in their life – second only to buying their own home. And yet car-makers seem to put car security pretty low on their list of priorities.
>
> We can't publicly blow the whistle on the specific design weaknesses we find in doors and locks, for fear of worsening the crime rate. But the makers know the problems as well as we do. They should be making doors more secure, protecting the ignition system and fitting an alarm system as standard (or, at least, offering it as an option). Latest figures suggest that more action could be taken to combat car crime. Manufacturers should act now.

Q Which is a fact and which is an opinion?

'For just £1 a week you can sponsor an abandoned dog.'

'Now isn't that a pound well spent?'

PRACTICE

The extract below contains both facts and opinions. List four examples of each.

Car Alarms

How they raise the alarm
The alarms set off either the car's horn or their own sounder – a horn or siren. Using the car's horn might be a bit of a risk if the thief is familiar with the car – he could open the bonnet and cut the horn connections. A siren is a distinctive sound – people nearby might take notice more quickly. Flashing headlights and indicators, are likely to raise eyebrows, especially at night.

Does it immobilise the car?
Many alarms also knock out the car's ignition. This is obviously a worthwhile protection – if a thief knocks out the horn he may still be unable to drive off.

What triggers the alarm?
Alarms can be triggered by vibrations made by a thief before the door is opened, a door being opened, or by something inside (the thief's movement, or by the engine being started, for example). The sooner the alarm goes off, the better.

How persistent is the alarm?
Many of the alarms go off only for a limited time after some sort of disturbance – which is sensible as it avoids too much unnecessary rumpus. Most importantly, all the vibration alarms stop after a while if accidentally triggered. But a cut-off could be bad if it left the car exposed after the thief's initial attack – some alarms stop even if the door is still open.

Security against alarm being switched off
The alarm's switch is a weak point. Perhaps the weakest is a key switch outside the car that can be picked easily. Many alarms are worked by a flick switch inside – totally vulnerable once found, though the thief would have to brazen out the noise while looking.

How convenient?
Simple flick switches are quite convenient. A few systems work with the car's ignition switch – even more convenient.

False alarming?
A car alarm that goes off unnecessarily, because the car is buffeted by gusts of wind, say, can drive people nearby to distraction. Some alarms are more prone to accidental triggering than others.

Following an argument

THE BARE BONES

➤ To follow an argument you need to understand and explain the main points in a text.

➤ The ability to follow an argument is a very important skill when answering exam questions.

A *How to follow an argument*

KEY FACT

When presenting their argument or point of view, writers use both <u>facts</u> and <u>opinions</u>.

For example:

One writer might argue that the minimum age for legally buying fireworks should be raised due to an increasing number of firework accidents among young people. To make this argument, the writer might include **facts** about the dangers of fireworks, as well as their own **opinion** of the irresponsible behaviour of young people.

B *How to spot the development of an argument*

1 Read the whole passage.

2 Underline the key words and phrases that reveal the writer's opinion.

3 Look out for facts that support this opinion.

4 Work out the different stages of the argument. Does the writer's opinion change throughout the text?

- Read through the article below, which presents one woman's view about putting her mother into a residential home for old people.

- In the first part, she reveals the **difficulties** she has in caring for her mother and her **worries** about putting her into a home.

Q Underline the words and phrases that reveal the writer's difficulties and worries.

Is it fair to put Mum in a home?

Mum is 88, and she'd lived in West London for 53 years before she had a fall in April this year and was taken into hospital. I'd always worried that if she needed more care, I couldn't cope at home. She needs lots of help, but wouldn't want me to give up my career. It would be impossible for her to live with us – our house is too small.

But all the guilt and the social pressures are horrendous. A lot of people are shocked that I could even think about putting my mother in a home.

Mum hates hospitals, and her mental state was deteriorating when she first went in. She had another fall in hospital, but then she was transferred to a terrific rehabilitation ward.

The social workers there said Mum's needs would be assessed to see what sort of care she required. I was scared she'd need nursing care – a lot of people in nursing homes are very confused, and I was worried that Mum would be put in a room full of mad people.

B

Can you spot the sentence that marks the turning point in the writer's argument?

• Now read the rest of the article and list the positive results of putting her mother in a home.

> I started looking at homes, and the one I'm hoping Mum will go to looks excellent. We're still waiting for the final assessment and for the council to agree that this particular home is right for Mum.
>
> Before she had her fall I knew she needed help, but I couldn't persuade her to take it. Now I know she'll be well cared for, her meals will be cooked for her and she'll have people around her, and we've actually become closer as a result of her fall.

• In the next example – a report from the *Guardian* newspaper – the writer comments on various points of view related to the changing world.

Remember

Read the questions first and underline key words.

Always answer in your own words and back up your answer with evidence from the article.

Queen, 71, bemoans trials of modern life

Jamie Wilson on varied reactions to the monarch's reflections

She may have her own internet site, and was jetting around the world before most people had ever been airborne, but yesterday the Queen confessed that she found it hard to keep up with the modern world.

The 71-year-old monarch, who is in Pakistan on the second day of her state visit, told the country's parliament: "I sometimes sense that the world is changing almost too fast for its inhabitants, at least for us older ones."

Her comments drew support from a number of her more elderly subjects. Veteran writer and broadcaster Ludovic Kennedy said he agreed entirely: "What she has said is absolutely right. For old dogs like us, new tricks are simply unacceptable."

Mr Kennedy, 77, continued: "The world is changing so fast we just can't keep pace with it.

"That is something older people have to accept."

Romantic novelist Dame Barbara Cartland, 95, echoed the Queen's sentiments, saying: "The world is changing too fast. The Queen is right, we need to get back to the way we were in the past.

"We need to get back to a previous age, where men behaved like gentlemen and women were women and not so busy building their careers. I think that is what

the Queen was trying to say and I agree with her."

However, Tony Benn, the 72-year-old Labour MP, felt one change was long overdue.

"The one thing that has not changed in my lifetime is the monarchy. If we could move into the next century with an elected head of state I would feel optimistic," he said.

But it was not all pessimism at the fast rate of progress. Betty Felsted from St Albans, a 70-year-old member of the Women's League of Health and Beauty, said that old people were sometimes blinded by science but that should not stop them from trying to keep up. "Just before I retired I learned how to use a word processor and I have no problem with video recorders or washing machines: I just read the instructions and get on with it.

"I always have a go at anything that comes along."

But Age Concern spokesman Margaret McLellan was sympathetic to the Queen's remarks, saying: "Many elderly people will feel the same way as the Queen.

"Feeling too old to catch up with the modern world can begin when people are as young as 40 or 50, and it is a feeling which gets worse as people get older."

PRACTICE

1 What point is the Queen making about modern life?

2 How does Ludovic Kennedy support and extend the Queen's point of view?

3 Look again at Barbara Cartland's views on the changing world. In what ways are her arguments different from those of Ludovic Kennedy?

4 What does Tony Benn's contribution add to the argument?

5 In what way do Betty Felsted's arguments disagree with some of the previous statements?

6 Out of all the views presented in this article, which is the closest to the views of the Queen? Explain why.

THE BARE BONES
➤ The purpose is the reason(s) why a text is written.
➤ The audience is the intended reader(s) or viewer(s).

A *Identifying the purpose of a text*

The purpose of a text is the reason why it was written. You need to ask yourself: **Why** was it written? Was it written to:

> ● inform   ● entertain   ● explain   ● advise   ● instruct   ● persuade
> ● for some other reason?

Sometimes texts can be written for more than one purpose. For example, an advertisement can be written to inform and persuade.

Q Can you think of two reasons why a newspaper article might be written?

> **You can work out the purpose of a text by studying its <u>features</u>.**

KEY FACT

- Look closely and underline the sections of the text which match the features in the green boxes.

> Manchester United confidently expect Louis Saha to become their third signing in a week after the French striker revealed last night that Fulham had told him he could go. The 25-year-old revealed the fee would be £10m and described himself as 'very happy', adding that joining the Premiership leaders would be 'like a dream'.

Features

- use of a variety of facts
- direct expression of feelings
- clear, accessible vocabulary, especially verbs

- These features tell you that the purpose of this text is **to inform**.

- Read the text below, which has been written **to persuade**:

> Morocco contains some of the most spectacular scenery in North Africa, ranging from the coniferous forests and snow-capped mountains of the Atlas to the hot sand and stone deserts of the Sahara. Most towns and villages on this itinerary are memorable in one way or another – from the remarkably sited city of Fes wedged in a valley, its houses climbing up the slope on either side – to the ancient walled city of Marrakech where Sir Winston Churchill loved to paint.

Features

- begins with clear statement of the attraction
- uses details of various features
- uses a wide range of descriptive vocabulary
- mentions an association with a famous person

Q Can you find examples in the text of each of these features?

B   *Identifying the audience*

To identify the audience for a text, you need to ask yourself:

> Who was it written for? Was it written for an adult, teenager or child, or a combination of these? Was it written for someone with a particular interest?

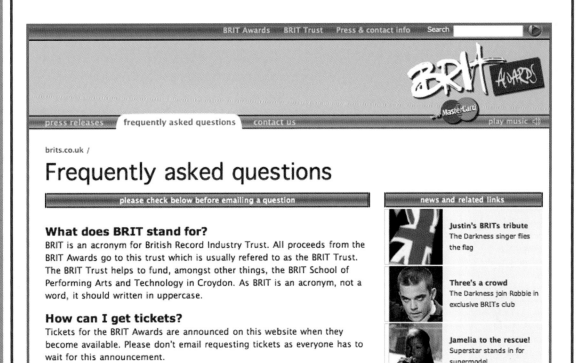

PRACTICE

Read the text below. What is the purpose of this text? How can you tell?

Comment on how the subject matter and the language give clues about the purpose.

What sort of person would read this? Give reasons for your answer.

SAVED
– THANKS TO RSPCA SUPPORTERS

Without the help of animal lovers like you, the RSPCA would be powerless in the war against cruelty and suffering. See for yourself how your donation can help save the lives of animals who have known only fear, pain and suffering.

Locked in a room for weeks without food, 10-year-old retriever Oliver was just half his recommended weight when the RSPCA found him. The vet said Oliver would have been dead within two days if we hadn't rescued him. Now fully recovered thanks to the dedicated care of RSPCA staff, Oliver has finally found the loving home he deserves.

THE BARE BONES

➤ To understand presentation you need to examine the appearance of a text.

➤ To evaluate presentation you need to comment on the visual effectiveness of the text.

In exam answers, you will be asked to comment on the effect and impact of the <u>appearance of texts</u>. This is known as the <u>layout</u>.

Layout refers to the type of print used, the pictures or illustrations and the way in which they are used in the text to <u>get the reader's attention</u>.

Remember
In an exam, you could be asked to explain how the layout helps the reader to understand the message of a text.

Here are some of the most commonly used presentational devices.

1 Headlines
The use of **bold lettering,** **capital letters** and an **exclamation mark** makes the headline appear dramatic and eye-catching.

In this headline, the question mark gives you something to think about.

The pound sign and the number attract your attention here.

DIRTY WATER KILLS!

Have you got what it takes?

£10 BUYS A CHAIN CUTTER

No time to draw breath?

2 Different sorts of print
Often a text will use different sizes of print and different **font styles** to draw attention to particular points.

The web page that follows uses bold print and a range of print sizes. Some information is written in very small print.
Why do you think advertisers sometimes choose to put information in small print?

Q What do you notice about the presentation here? How does the presentation help to get the message across?

1 What is the purpose of the top line of the web page?

2 What is the purpose of the box on the left-hand side headed 'Holiday search'?

3 What impact do you think is made by the pictures?

4 How might the pictures affect the reader's response to this website?

Make a
st of logos
nat you see
very day.

PRACTICE

Read the text below.

1 How many different types of print can you identify?

2 How is print type used to emphasise the message of this text?

3 How do the pictures link with the written text?

4 How might the pictures affect the reader's response to this advertisement?

Oxfam
FREEPOST (OF 353)
274 Banbury Road
Oxford OX2 7BR

*Help them build a
future free from
hunger and disease*

How does Oxfam make your £2 work so hard?

How can we possibly make just £2 do so much?

The answer lies in the effort, the determination, and the ingenuity of the people we help.

Oxfam doesn't walk into a Third World country with ready-made solutions, or quick-fix answers. We work alongside local people, and help them work out solutions that suit their individual circumstances.

The projects Oxfam supports are always carefully monitored, so that money isn't wasted, and worthwhile lessons can be applied elsewhere.

Oxfam supports 3,000 projects in over 70 countries worldwide.

...for just £2 a month.

**Your £2 a month will help these people in their daily struggle to help themselves.
Please complete the coupon inside.**

THE BARE BONES

➤ Writers match the language they use to their audience and purpose.

➤ The type of language used in a text affects the way the reader receives the message.

➤ Evaluating the language of a text means explaining the impact that the language has on the reader.

Types of language

1 Dramatic or emotive language

Dramatic or emotive language is used to attract the reader's attention, especially in newspaper headlines.

> **Hospitals face crisis over fatal fall in blood supplies**

KEY FACT

> **Emotive language** is language that is intended to arouse strong feelings.

In the example above, the word 'crisis' suggests that this is a very serious situation. This is further emphasised by the use of the word 'fatal'. Both words would make readers want to read on.

2 Imperatives

KEY FACT

> **Imperatives** are words that give **instructions** or **orders**.

Imperatives are used to appeal directly to the reader and to make the message very clear. In this example, the word 'discover' is being used as an imperative.

> **DISCOVER**
> Your *FAVOURITE* days out in
> **CHESHIRE**

Q What sort of texts do you think are most likely to use imperatives?

3 Alliteration

This is where writers use the same sound to start several words in a headline, as in the example. It's a common way of catching the reader's attention.

> **Ringway rumpus**
> POLICE were called to Manchester Airport

4 Questions

Questions are used by writers to get the reader involved directly. They have the same effect as the use of imperatives – they make you think the writer is talking to you personally.

> **What choice will *YOU* make?**

5 Colloquial language

Colloquial language is informal. It is the language of everyday conversation and is used to make it easy for readers to relate to the text. In the text 'How green are you?', there are several examples of colloquial speech; for example, 'Hands up'. This makes the text easy to read and so gets the message across.

This article starts with the question, 'How green are you?' What effect does this question have on the reader?

Can you find four examples of colloquial language in the text opposite?

PRACTICE

How green are you?

Hands up if you have recently done any of the following:

- thrown a glass bottle in the rubbish bin;
- left the tap running while cleaning your teeth;
- poured cooking oil down the drain;
- flushed cotton wool down the loo;
- left the fridge door open while paying the milkman;
- thrown away plastic carriers from the back of a cupboard;
- heated the oven to bake a solitary spud.

Yes, me too. On the other hand, I do recycle bottles, cans and paper, and take clothes to charity shops, so I thought I was doing pretty well, until I started working on this supplement.

Who can put their hand on their heart and honestly say that they always make the greenest decisions about their home?

Friday October 24

Community News

Ninja peril of Black Lake

Dumped terrapins decimate wildlife

An exotic pet which grows from the dimensions of a 50p piece into a plate-sized monster is causing havoc among wildlife after being dumped illegally in a Wilmslow pool.

There are thought to be dozens of American reared terrapins – left-overs of the Ninja Mutant Turtle craze – in Black Lake on Lindow Common.

The 12in-diameter creatures gobble up insects, newts, frogs and even baby water birds. Experts say that unless the terrapins can be curbed local wildlife will be devastated.

The problem began when the terrapins were dumped after they became too big to handle in household aquariums.

The wily reptiles are proving difficult to catch. So far, they have dodged all efforts at trapping.

1 What impression is given of the terrapins in this article?

2 How does the language of the headline and subheading help to emphasise this impression?

3 Choose five words and phrases from the text that you think have been used for dramatic effect. For each one, explain why you think it is dramatic and what readers will think when they read these particular words.

Comparing texts

THE BARE BONES

➤ In exams, you are often asked to write in detail about <u>similarities</u> and <u>differences</u> between two texts.

➤ You will be asked to compare: the content of the texts, the writers' purposes, the way information is presented, the way language is used and the way in which the texts appeal to their intended audience(s).

A The content of a text

KEY FACT

The <u>content</u> means <u>what that text is about</u>. You are expected to write two or three lines to summarise what the text tells you.

Q Look at the texts opposite. Complete these sentences:

Text A is about ....

Text A tells the reader ....

Text B is about ...

Text B tells the reader ...

Both texts give the reader an impression of Cyprus that is ...

Note that the comparison of the texts comes in the last sentence and is signalled by the word 'both'.

Text A

Discover Hidden Treasure in the Mediterranean

NORTH CYPRUS is a charmed land. A land where you can get away from the crowds and discover miles of deserted beaches, golden sandy beaches. Where you can walk in beautiful mountains, home to rare species of plant and wildlife. A land with a history almost as long as civilisation itself, with a treasure trove of castles, abbeys and palaces, which you can explore at will. An enchanting land where a holiday will feel like a fairy tale.

Text B

The Land I Love

One of my earliest memories is walking beside my grandfather in the mountains of Cyprus following our herd of sheep as they climbed higher and higher up the mountain through the **lush green grass** and the **scented wild flowers**. In the middle of the day we used to shelter from the burning sun under large fig trees. If I try hard enough I still can conjure up the taste of their **sweet juicy flesh**.

When we came down from the mountain we used to stop at the well for a drink of the coolest water. In those days Greek and Turkish Cypriots got on well together and we children used to play games in the dusty streets.

On **cold wet days** in the northern industrial town where I now live, my thoughts still wander back to **hot sunny days** in the land I love.

B The writer's purpose

KEY FACT

The <u>purpose</u> of a text is the <u>reason it was written</u>. Sometimes texts can be written for <u>more than one purpose</u>.

Q Explain the purpose(s) of Text A and Text B.

Study this list of purposes for writing:

● to entertain ● to describe ● to argue ● to inform ● to persuade ● to advise.

C The way information is presented

When you are asked to **compare** and **contrast** the presentation of a text, look at the following:

- use of headlines and subheadings
- the way paragraphs are arranged
- how the presentation matches the purpose of the text.
- type and size of font
- use of illustration

D The way language is used

These are useful **sentence starters** when you are writing to **compare** and **contrast**:

- Both texts . . . ● They are similar because . . . ● Similarly . . . ● In the same way . . .
- They are different because . . . ● On the other hand . . . ● In contrast to . . .

When you **compare** and **contrast** the language of each text, comment on:

- the type of language the writer uses (for example, is it positive or negative?)

- the reason why the writer has used this sort of language

- the way in which words are placed together; for example, several adjectives used one after the other for maximum impact

- the effect that the language has on the reader; what the reader thinks when reading the text.

E The way in which the texts appeal to their audience

Sometimes, in an exam, you may be asked to compare the likely appeal of two texts. To do this you need to think about how well content, presentation and language target the intended purpose and audience.

1 Compare and contrast the ways Texts A and B are presented. Explain how the layout of each helps to put across its message.

2 Compare and contrast the ways in which language is used in Texts A and B. In particular, refer to the highlighted parts of each text.

PRACTICE

Compare the different ways Text A and Text B present Cyprus as an attractive place. In your answer you should write about:

- what the writers are trying to achieve

- the ways the texts are presented

- the ways the language is used to influence the reader.

THE BARE BONES

➤ When writing, it is very important to match your vocabulary, content and sentence structure to the needs of the reader.
➤ Different types of reader need different styles of writing.

KEY FACT

Q Can you find any more examples of places where the writer has matched their style to meet the needs of the audience – in this case, children?

Remember
Use 'you' to address the reader and ask questions to involve the reader.

Q What do you notice about the vocabulary and sentence structure in 'What makes a good friend?' What evidence is there to show that this text has been written to match the needs of an older audience?

Think about the needs of your reader(s) (your <u>audience</u>) when you are planning your work.

Look at this piece of writing, which is aimed at children. Notice that the vocabulary and sentence structure are simple so they can easily be read and understood.

Bicycles

bicycle compared with children's toys

vocabulary repeated – only one idea in a sentence

The first bicycle was a <u>sort of</u> <u>hobby-horse</u> on wheels. It had no pedals so you had to push it forward like a scooter. It was impossible to steer.

You could steer this bicycle by turning the handle-bars. But you still had to push it along with your feet.

This was one of the first bicycles with <u>pedals</u>. <u>Pedalling</u> was very hard work. The <u>pedals</u> went backwards and forwards and drove the back wheel.

informal language

use of You to involve the reader

- Study the extract below, which was written for a teenage audience.
- Using the information in the article, as well as your own ideas, write a paragraph entitled 'Choosing a friend' for a PSHEC textbook.

What makes a good friend?

A friend should be...

Funny   Lazy   Daring   Helpful

Hard-working   Serious

Intelligent   Rebellious   Shy

1 What do you look for in a friend? Do you want someone to laugh with or someone to share your troubles? Do you want someone to moan to about problems with teachers or homework? With a partner, make a list of all the things you look for in a friend.

2 What makes a good friend? Look closely at the qualities in this list. Work with a partner to put the qualities into three categories under these headings:
Very important to me
Fairly important
Not important at all.

- Suggest other qualities not included in the list, but which you think are important.

- The extract below is taken from an article written for an adult audience about teenage gambling.

One-armed bandits

opening statement introduces topic of text →

For many teenagers the lure of the fruit machines is irresistible. The combination of noise, lights and cash incentives make them an attractive form of escapism. However, many experts now see them as increasingly responsible for the growing number of teenage gamblers. 'Fruit machines are a form of hard gambling,' says Dr Emmanuel Moran of the National Council of Gambling. 'They are compulsive and habit forming.'

marker introduces new point →

marker introduces new point →

In fact, a survey, carried out by the National Housing and Town Planning Council, suggested that more than 300,000 British teenagers spend their school dinner money on fruit machines. Over 130,000 are stealing money from their parents to finance their obsession.

- You will see that this text has been annotated to show you something about the structure of the text.

Markers are used in a text to show that a new point is being introduced.

Y FACT

PRACTICE

1 Write a short paragraph to explain one of the following to a younger child:
  - how to make a cup of tea
  - why children have to go to school.

2 Write a short article aimed at alerting parents to the dangers of teenage gambling.

  Here are some ideas to help you:
  - It is believed that the problem of teenage gambling is growing ...
  - Fruit machines are becoming attractive to teenagers because ...
  - Gambling is habit-forming ...

Planning your writing

THE BARE BONES

➤ In the exam, you'll be asked to produce writing that argues, persuades or advises, or that explains, informs or describes.

➤ You will be expected to write in a range of different forms, such as letters, leaflets, articles, reports or speeches.

➤ You will be expected to write for a particular audience in a way that gets your message across.

A What skills do I need?

You are expected to:

- plan your work so that the finished piece of writing is well organised

- match your writing to your audience and purpose

- organise your ideas into sentences and paragraphs

- vary the length and style of your sentences

- use a wide range of vocabulary that is suitable for the task

- present your work clearly and neatly using legible handwriting

- use correct punctuation

- spell correctly.

Remember
You should spend at least five minutes planning and sequencing your ideas.

B Planning your writing

KEY FACT

Examiners give credit for work that is well structured and logical, so spend time planning your work before you start writing.

Decide what you are going to say, how you are going to say it and in what order you will present it. Make a simple plan – just a few key words or sentences to help you organise what you want to say.

Remember
Don't forget to match your content, vocabulary and sentence structure to the needs of your audience and the purpose of your task.

C Presentation

Different types of writing need different types of presentation:

- Letters need appropriate beginnings and endings.

- Articles need headlines and subheadings.

- Leaflets need a variety of fonts and different styles of presentation, such as bullet points, to make it easy for the reader to access information quickly.

D Paragraphs

Dividing your ideas into paragraphs helps the reader to follow your argument.

- Generally, you should put all your ideas on the same topic in one paragraph.
- Stop writing every few minutes and read what you have written to see if you need to begin a new paragraph.

E Punctuation

- Punctuation helps the reader to understand. Think about where you place commas, full stops, question marks, exclamation marks, apostrophes and ellipses (...).
- Go back every few sentences to check your punctuation.

F Spelling

Correct spelling is crucial in writing exams. Revise spellings before the exam and make use of spelling rules in your English textbooks.

- Make a note of words that you often get wrong and make a special effort to learn them.
- Pin them up near your desk so you can see them as you do your revision.

G Writing under exam conditions

1 Always spend a few minutes reading the questions. Make your choice carefully so that you know exactly what type of writing is required. Highlight key question words.

2 Make a plan before you begin writing. This could take the form of a spidergram, a chart or a series of bullet points.

3 Think through each sentence before you write it.

4 Read your work through as you are writing. Research shows that this practice helps students to stay focused on purpose and audience.

Read this paragraph, which has been written in exam conditions. Can you spot and correct the mistakes? Can you think of ways to make it more interesting?

Ever since I was little I have been intrested in cylcling. My first bike had extra weels to help me balance but I soon graduatd to a bmx I used to where bald patches in the lawn doing my stunts.

THE BARE BONES

➤ When you write to argue you are trying to impress your readers with your point of view.

➤ Look for opportunities to use emotive and loaded vocabulary to make your points effectively.

KEY POINT

Q How many facts and how many opinions can you find for both 'Yes' and 'No' in the text below?

Remember
Aim to make the reader share your views by using the words 'we' and 'us'.

When you write to argue, you are getting your readers to accept your point of view.

- When you write to argue, you include **facts** as well as **opinions** to convince your readers.

- Read the text below. Two opposing points of view are presented here. Some of the features of **writing to argue** have been labelled for you.

reader involved directly

facts to support argument

Fireworks: time for a total ban?

YES Let's bring an end to the dangers of fireworks, and impose a total ban on the things once and for all. This newspaper has already highlighted how a new law banning the sale of dangerous fireworks to children is being ignored by some shop owners in Greater Manchester. Even organised displays aren't safe, as was proved last night, when people, including children, were injured at a display in the West Midlands.

Every year in the build-up to Bonfire Night, Postbag publishes letters from people who are sick and tired of hearing fireworks being let off in their area weeks before November 5. Youngsters terrorise old people and those with pets.

Every year people are maimed and even killed by fireworks, despite all the government's efforts to warn of the dangers. Thoughtless idiots will always ignore the warnings, and innocent people will be hurt, unless we ban all fireworks now.

NO Talk of banning all fireworks is an over-reaction. It is true that people are hurt by them, but nothing can be made completely safe these days, not even crossing the road! For many years fireworks and bonfires have brought lots of enjoyment to generations of people in this country. It is one winter's night when everybody gets out and about and has fun. Banning fireworks would put a lot of people out of work, for one thing. And you could hardly ban fireworks without forbidding people to build bonfires. How on earth could such a ban be imposed?

Last night's display was an unfortunate accident, and people were hurt, but it was a one-off. The vast majority of such displays are safe, and there is no earthly reason why they should not continue to be so. Let us not deny children the pleasure that Fireworks Night can bring.

emotive language

rhetorical question

final opinions clearly stated

Structuring your ideas is an essential part of writing to argue.
You will need a good supply of **connecting words**. These will help you to:

- string ideas together
- make comparisons with differing points of view.

Here are a few to get you started.

implies that *so*

however *on the other hand* *because*

suggests *on the one hand* *whereas* *therefore*

Use appropriate connecting words to link the strings of ideas below.

A School meals are now full of unhealthy foods – children are becoming overweight – we should return to old fashioned, no choice, two course school dinners – parents should take more responsibility for what children eat.

B The internet is full of possible cheats for GCSE coursework – assessment should be by examination only – most students are honest and work hard – exams don't suit everyone.

C Gym membership will keep you fit – you need professional advice before you start – gym membership should be free to everyone – gyms don't develop team spirit.

KEY POINT

Think about your overall structure.

- Introduce your subject clearly and forcefully.
- Whether you are arguing for or against something, you need to have a series of strong points supported by relevant facts and/or personal experience.
- When developing your argument, show you are aware of the opposite point of view. Use phrases such as: 'It could be argued that...' to introduce these. Make counter arguments against these.
- End with a positive conclusion. You could make a new point at the very end to leave your reader thinking.

PRACTICE

1 Write the notes for your contribution to a class debate in your Citizenship class in which you **argue** that Premiership footballers are vastly overpaid.

2 Write an article for a school magazine in which you either agree or disagree with a ban on fireworks. Your **purpose** is to present a clear **argument** for your ideas.

3 Write a letter to your local council in which you **argue** for the improvements in the facilities for under-16s in your area.

THE BARE BONES

➤ When you write to persuade, you aim to make your reader believe something, agree with something or do something.

➤ You need to use language to get the reader on your side.

When you write to persuade, you are trying to get your readers to do something.

Writing to persuade includes the following features:

- direct appeal to the reader using questions and/or the pronoun 'you'

- language used emotively to appeal to the feelings of readers

- punctuation designed to get the reader's attention (e.g. exclamation marks).

The Albert Dock
Liverpool

Exciting shopping!

For shopping that's different, there is nowhere quite like the Albert Dock.

■ Undercover malls house scores of small, individual shops and brightly coloured coster carts displaying an amazing range of merchandise.

■ From toys to treasures, candy to clocks, books to baseball caps, the Dock's got the lot!

■ Fashion-seekers of all ages are well-provided for, with shops selling ladies', men's and children's fashions. Accessories? You'll find no shortage of jewellery, scarves, bags and fragrances to go with that new designer outfit.

■ Souvenir hunting? The Dock can hardly be bettered. There's a staggering range of Beatles mementoes along with items commemorating those other local heroes, Liverpool and Everton Football Clubs. And in between there's everything from a picture postcard or guidebook of the Albert Dock to ships' clocks and other reminders of the city's proud maritime past. "Shop at the Dock" – it's all part of the irresistible Albert Dock experience!

Q How many examples of the features of writing to persuade can you find in this text?

When writing to persuade you must keep your audience in mind.

You need to make sure your readers know you understand their point of view. You should also think of the language and punctuation features you need to use to help persuade your audience.

Look at the following text:

Westport is a nice town by the seaside. It has a long promenade which is kept clean by the busy local council workers. The promenade has many smashing flower displays which are looked after by the gardeners.

The beach has a lot of yellow sand and it is safe to swim in the sea.

The local theatres have a lot of entertainment in the summer. The local golf club will allow visitors to play and the sports centre will give visitors temporary membership. There are also some clubs for young people who want to stay up late.

Q Underline or highlight the adjectives and verbs in this text.

Q Write the text again, changing the adjectives and verbs to create a more attractive picture of Westport.

Would this text succeed in persuading its readers to take a holiday or a short break in Westport? Probably not!

It does not use language to persuade. Look at the **adjectives** and **verbs**.

These should be the key persuasive words. They should make people feel excited and eager to visit Westport.

Compare:

> Westport is a nice town by the seaside.

with

> Westport shimmers as a jewel of a town by the seaside.

Compare:

> It has a long promenade.

with

> It boasts an extensive promenade.

Think also of the punctuation. Rewrite one sentence so that it ends with an exclamation mark. Rewrite a different sentence so that it becomes a rhetorical question.

KEY FACT

Picking words that affect the feelings of your audience is vital.

Imagine you are campaigning against a plan by your local council to open a new youth centre. You are trying to persuade local residents to vote against it by making them worried about possible noise and vandalism.

Here are some useful words and phrases you could use:

graffiti   a disgrace   hordes of young troublemakers   disturbing our peace

outrageous   nightmare   asking for trouble

Remember Choose words that will have a direct effect on your reader.

Can you think of some more?

PRACTICE

Write a leaflet based on your town or a place that you have visited. Your **purpose** is to **persuade** readers to visit the place you have chosen.

You should:

- give a range of details about the place
- appeal directly to your reader
- choose adjectives and verbs to make it sound attractive
- use one or two exclamations and/or rhetorical questions for effect.

Writing to advise

➤ When writing to advise, it is important to match your vocabulary, content and sentence structure to the needs of the reader.

➤ Different readers respond to advice in different ways.

A *Looking at language*

Q How many imperatives can you find in this text? Find one other way the writer has used to present advice.

1 Some advice sheets use a series of instructions to give advice.

Look at this example:

GETTING INTO GOOD HABITS

● Aim to use less of everything. Stick to instructions and hold back on that extra squirt.

● Ask yourself whether the sink really needs another clean or whether clothes can be aired rather than washed.

● Cleaning products work better in soft water, so you can use less. If you live in a hard-water area, use a softener.

● Do you really need individual cleaners for the different parts of your home?

● Stop buying aerosols, even if they don't contain CFCs.

2 Sometimes advice leaflets use facts to advise readers.

Look at this example:

Q List the facts, supported by figures, used in this advice leaflet.

Most parents, quite rightly, worry about their children trying drugs. They want to know the risks and what to do if they suspect their child is using drugs. But – as many teachers, hospital staff and police officers will tell you – alcohol can cause just as many problems for young people. One thousand children under the age of 15 are admitted to hospital each year with acute alcohol poisoning. Around half of pedestrians aged between 16 and 60 killed in road accidents have more alcohol in their blood than the legal drink drive limit. In 1994, 57,800 people were found guilty or cautioned for drunkenness. The peak age of offenders was 18.

3 Sometimes writers adopt a friendly tone to get readers on their side and to encourage them to take the advice.

Q What features of this writing help the readers to feel that the writer is friendly towards them?

Text messages or phone calls – bullying in the 21st century

If you repeatedly receive unpleasant or threatening messages, keep a record and tell an adult – even if you know who it is. If it is bullying, it needs dealing with. Remember that seeming upset will show your aggressors that they are winning. Walk tall and be confident. Ignore nasty comments and insults.

Q How has the writer shown understanding of the problems of the readers? Find at least three examples.

When you write to advise, you are persuading someone to do something.

- It is important to get your audience on your side so that they will take your advice.

- You should show that you understand their feelings and reassure them about their difficulties.

HAVE YOU JUST STARTED SECONDARY SCHOOL?

Beginning a new term at school can be a very daunting experience. Your new school will probably be much bigger than your old one and you may worry about finding your way around.

Remember you are not on your own – there are lots of people who will help you. You can ask a teacher or an older student to show you the way if you get lost.

Learning lots of new subjects can be confusing too. Some new students find it hard to remember all of their books and equipment in the first few weeks. It is a good idea to pack your bag the night before and to check your diary to make sure that you have everything you need.

Imagine that a friend of yours has asked your advice on meeting coursework deadlines at GCSE. Problems with coursework have led to extra difficulties with routine homework and classwork. List the points you could make when offering advice to your friend. How would you show you understand how they are feeling? Remember that good, well-written advice will not only deal with a problem, but will also point out the benefits of following that advice.

Your school wants to run a breakfast club for GCSE students. Use the chart below to list the problems and the positive advantages of a breakfast club.

Problems	Advantages of a breakfast club

Now use one of the problems and one of the advantages to help you write one paragraph of advice on running a breakfast club.

PRACTICE

1 Write three paragraphs for a booklet called 'Settling in at Secondary School'. Your **purpose** is to **advise** Year 7 students.

2 Your school library has now been up-dated to the highest standards with both books and IT facilities. Write an advice sheet, to be posted in the library, which will help new Year 7 students use the facilities to help their school work.

3 Write the text of a leaflet which will be sent to older people in your community giving them advice on a healthy diet and lifestyle.

THE BARE BONES

➤ Effective writing to inform demands that you concentrate on giving full details to your readers.

➤ You must plan the organisation of your information carefully.

A Using detail

To do well in this type of writing in the exam you will be expected to use a wide range of detail in your information.

It will be important to plan your work, both by noting down the details you are going to use and then deciding the **sequence** in which you are going to use that detail.

Here is a list of facilities and benefits – a list of points of information which might feature in the publicity for a local sports centre.

Wide range of sporting activities available – swimming, badminton, weight training, etc.	Low cost membership with a variety of discounts (e.g. family membership; special rates for those on benefits).
All activities supervised at all times by qualified staff.	Free car parking in large supervised car park.
Specialist coaching available in many activities.	Regular and cheap public transport links from town centre.
Specialist advice available for beginners to get started.	Opportunities to represent the centre in team and individual sports.
Variety of times available to suit working parents, single parents, etc.	Café, bistro and licensed bar available; can be booked for social events.

Q Which details of this information will make the writing most effective?

Imagine you have to write an effective information sheet on the sports centre to be used as an insert in your local free newspaper. Use numbers to work out the sequence to give this variety of detailed information in its most effective form.

This type of information is **impersonal**. But there will be opportunities to use **personal** information in this type of writing.

Many local newspapers now feature local residents as their Personality of the Week – or operate similar features. What information would you need if you were going to write about someone known to you for this type of feature. Would it include aspects of their life? Their particular contributions to local life? Their feelings about their local community?

Write out some brief notes on someone you could feature in this type of writing.

Now think of the best **sequence**.

Remember
Aim to use a variety of details and to sequence them effectively.

Remember it is a newspaper article; you need to grab the reader's attention in the first paragraph.

Choose the section of your notes which would do this best and write out your opening paragraph.

B Reporting issues

Reports about issues often give information about a recent happening. Their main purpose is to inform readers.

Read this example closely:

Hitting out

Should parents be allowed to smack their children? Emily Moore looks at the issues.

A 12-year-old boy won the right to go to the European Court of Human Rights in Strasbourg last week because his stepfather beat him with a garden cane when he was nine years old. The hearing may take two years – if the boy wins, smacking could be banned in Britain.

Does British law allow grown-ups to hit children?
Yes it does. Parents have the right to use what is called "reasonable chastisement" to keep their children under control (1933 Children and Young Person's Act). So, parents may hit them, but not hard enough to cause serious injury.

However, in 1991 the British government did agree to abide by Article 19 of the United Nations Convention of the Rights of the Child, which says children should be protected from all forms of physical or mental violence. The UN is "deeply worried" about British law which allows adults to hit children.

Do any countries ban smacking?
Physical punishment of children is illegal in Austria, Cyprus, Denmark, Finland, Norway and Sweden. Sweden banned it in 1979 and studies show that violence against children has declined in the 17 years since then.

Why do parents smack their children?
Most parents were smacked when they were children and some believe it is the best way to stop a child's bad behaviour. All children need to learn the difference between right and wrong – the question is, does smacking teach this?

1 What event is the starting-point for this report?

2 What issue is raised in this report?

3 How does the report use facts and figures to help the reader understand the issues?

4 How does the report draw the reader's attention to different aspects of the issue?

1 Using the information in the report above, write your own report on the topic of smacking children.
  - Before you begin, make a list of the points that you will include (you can use some of the information from the report above).
  - Start with the same information about the twelve-year-old boy.
  - Use subheadings to summarise the content of each paragraph.
  - Include comments from parents and children. You can make these up.

2 Write your own news report based on one of the following:
  - the decision by a local council to sell playing fields to make way for a motorway
  - gales and torrential rain that have caused damage to houses and flooding.

Pay careful attention to the use of detail and sequencing. Think carefully about the wording of your opening paragraph.

THE BARE BONES

➤ When writing to explain your aim is to answer the questions 'How?' and 'Why?'

➤ You need to select details carefully and concentrate on organisation and structure.

Remember
When you write to explain, you are answering the questions 'How?' and 'Why?'

If you choose to write in this style in the exam there will be some similarities to writing to **inform**. Use of detail and sequencing will again be very important.

But you will also need to show that you are aware of your reader's possible response and that, possibly, you can influence that response.

Also, in this style, it is far more possible for you to use anecdotes as well as linguistic features like satire, irony and humour. But remember that your anecdotes must be relevant and not rambling and that your humour must not be coarse or heavy-handed.

Imagine that you are being asked to write an article for your school newspaper explaining the particular pressures of the GCSE year.

Complete your own version of the table to help develop your explanation.

Particular pressure	Possible audience response
Enormous amounts of homework.	Happens in other years; also you need to be prepared for extra work in Sixth Form and beyond.

Now take one of the pressures, and its possible response, and write a paragraph to **explain** its effect on a GCSE student. Remember to try to deal with and influence the possible response in your paragraph.

Look at this extract from a newspaper article.

One judge said rhapsodically that the book had 'used disability to throw a light upon the world.'

The chairwoman, Joan Bakewell, called it, 'an absolutely fantastic book, quite exceptional in the way Haddon is able to express the voice of the child and to get into the boy's language. It is extraordinary because of the limitations he has put on himself. He manages to reveal the boy as a thinking and tender person.

We also thought it terribly funny. None of the judges has known anything like it.'

She added that the novel led readers to see through the boy the chaos of the adult world around him.

In the article, the writer is reporting the award to Mark Haddon's book *The Curious Incident of The Dog in The Night-time* as Whitbread Book of the Year. The story is centred around a boy with Asperger's syndrome, a form of autism that makes socialising with others very difficult.

Here two of the judges are explaining their decision. When you explain you give reasons. You answer the questions 'How?' and 'Why?'

What method is used in the article to present different opinions?

Features of the book	Reasons for selection
Tone	
Language	
Difficulties for the author	
Effect of using this boy as main character	
Overall effect on readers	

Now think of your favourite book. Select **four** features of it which make it special to you. Set them out in a table similar to that above.

Features of the book	Reasons for selection

PRACTICE

1 Explain why particular days or times of the year are particularly important to you and your family.
   In your answer you should write about:
   • the details of holidays or religious festivals or other important days
   • the details of why they particularly matter to you and your family
   • the effects on family life and the differing views of your friends.

2 Explain where you think the main influences today – in the attitudes of young people and the way they look and dress – come from.

THE BARE BONES

➤ Effective descriptive writing paints a picture in words without telling a story.

➤ You need to think of a structure which is not dependent on narrative.

If you choose to write to describe in the exam you will almost certainly describe a person or a place.

Look at this description from *Great Expectations* by Charles Dickens.

> *My sister, Mrs. Joe, with black hair and eyes, had such a prevailing redness of skin that I sometimes used to wonder whether it was possible she washed herself with a nutmeg grater instead of soap. She was tall and bony, and almost always wore a coarse apron, fastened over her figure behind with two loops, and having a square impregnable bib in front, that was stuck full of pins and needles.*

Pick out the words and phrases which make Mrs. Joe such an unattractive character.

Now look at this description from *Far from the Madding Crowd* by Thomas Hardy.

> *When Farmer Oak smiled, the corners of his mouth spread till they were within an unimportant distance of his ears, his eyes were reduced to chinks, and diverging wrinkles appeared around them, extending upon his countenance like the rays in a rudimentary sketch of the rising sun.*

Pick out the words and phrases which make Farmer Oak seem an attractive character.

You will notice that:

- Choices of **vocabulary** and **language features**, e.g. similes, are very important in effective description. For example: '*diverging wrinkles … like the rays … sun*'.

- Writers often use one aspect only of a character's appearance, e.g. Farmer Oak's smile or Mrs. Joe's skin and apron, to give a general picture of their appearance or character. This might be a useful strategy in the time constraints of an examination.

Vocabulary choices are also important when writing about a place. Notice how John Steinbeck has used well-chosen verbs and adjectives to give a peaceful view of nature in the opening lines in *Of Mice and Men*.

> *A few miles south of Soledad, the Salinas River drops in close to the hillside bank and runs deep and green. The water is warm too, for it has slipped twinkling over the yellow sands in the sunlight before reaching the narrow pool. On one side of the river the golden foothill slopes curve up to the strong and rocky Gabilan mountains, but on the valley side the water is lined with trees – willows fresh and green with every spring, carrying in their leaf junctures the debris of the winter's flooding; and sycamores with mottled, white, recumbent limbs and branches that arch over the pool.*

Q Underline words and phrases in the Steinbeck extract which you think are effective.

Notice how the description creates a clear **picture** of the place in your mind. This is the purpose of descriptive writing about a place. The mistake that many GCSE candidates make is to tell a story about a place rather than describing it.

For example, when asked to write a description of a busy town centre on a weekend evening some candidates would tell the story of a night out rather than writing a description.

One way round this problem is to think out a **structure** for your description, e.g. you could imagine yourself walking through a town centre and then paint the pictures in words of selected stages of your journey. Try to complete this table to help with organisation.

Point on Journey	Descriptive words or language features to use
Getting out of bus or taxi	
Scene around the main shops	
Scene around eating places	
Appearance of pubs, outside and inside	
Appearance of crowds in actual centre	
Less attractive places	
Contrast when going home	

When you are filling in the descriptive boxes remember that you will not just see things but also smell them, touch them, hear them and even, possibly, taste them.

Concentration on appropriate structure and selection of vocabulary is vital.

Write a paragraph plan for this exam question: 'Describe a noisy beach scene'.

Remember
Use your different senses when writing description.

KEY POINT

PRACTICE

Describe the scene in your school dining hall at lunchtime.

Remember to:

- plan the structure of your description. You could organise your description as though you were moving around the room with a video recorder
- focus on distinctive aspects of different people's appearance
- use a range of vocabulary and language features, such as similes, to make your description effective.

THE BARE BONES ➤ To express yourself clearly in writing you need to be aware of the conventions of punctuation and spelling.

A Writing in sentences

The examiners are looking for more than just correct punctuation. They are looking for you to vary the length and style of sentences to make your writing interesting and lively for the reader.

We will look at punctuation first.

KEY POINT ➤

> Remember that a sentence must make complete sense and end with either a full stop, a question mark or an exclamation mark.

Decide where the sentences end in this short paragraph and insert the correct end-of-sentence punctuation.

Where could her purse have got to it was nowhere to be found but then came a flash of inspiration

Notice how punctuation clarifies meaning here. That is why it is so important for you to write in correctly punctuated sentences in the exam. The examiner must understand your meaning to award an appropriate mark.

Now look at this piece of writing.

Q When should an exclamation mark be used at the end of a sentence?

Tom walked across the road. He preferred to walk although he had a trendy bike at home. He crossed the road as the clock struck ten. He was in good time for his meeting.

Here the sentences have been punctuated correctly but they lack variety. They all start with the subject '*Tom*' or the pronoun subject '*he*'. Yet two of the sentences have sub-clauses with the connectives '*although*' and '*as*'. Write the paragraph out again, putting the sub-clauses first. Notice the difference it makes to the writing.

Making a difference to the length of sentences by using connectives is a vital writing skill in the exam.

'*Although*' and '*as*' have been used above. Add as many as you can to the list. Try to remember their use in the exam.

B Writing in paragraphs

In the exam the paragraph structure of your writing will be very important. When to begin a new paragraph is more obvious in some types of writing, for example:
• when developing a new point in writing to argue or persuade
• when moving to a new set of instructions or a new topic in writing to advise.

But in other writing it depends upon how you want your work to develop. The key to success is in your **planning** before you start to write. If you list your ideas for your writing you can then **sequence** them. This will give you a paragraph order and a chance to change paragraphs around.

B

Here are two sets of notes. One is for descriptive writing about a favourite holiday destination and one is for informative writing about the attractions of your school.

Use numbers to put them in sequence to produce an effective paragraph structure.

DESCRIBE	INFORM
Lively nightlife	Well-qualified staff
Clean beaches	Many extra-curricular activities
Wide range of accommodation	Excellent examination results
Ease of access	Well-designed modern buildings
Wide range of restaurants	Excellent school meals
Wide range of shops	Strong pastoral care system

Notice that by planning and sequencing the paragraphing takes care of itself. Time spent on these activities before you start to write is not time wasted. It is better than starting to write immediately and then getting into a muddle with paragraphs and structure.

Remember
Planning and sequencing help you to paragraph effectively.

C *Use of speech in writing*

The use of actually spoken words can make writing very lively. It gives the writing realism and can often help if you want to present a character in a particular light. But you do need to punctuate it correctly to achieve maximum effect. Look at this conversation:

Note these features:

- **Speech marks** go around the words actually spoken.

- The first word spoken has a **capital letter** whether or not it is at the start of a sentence.

- Final sentence punctuation comes **inside** the last set of speech marks.

- **Commas** split off the words actually spoken from the rest of the sentence.

- When you introduce a different speaker you start a **new paragraph**.

- There are many alternatives to 'said'. Use them!

> Sandy picked the phone up and asked excitedly, 'Who is this?'
> Immediately came the reply, 'It's me, Kath.'
> 'I'm glad you've rung,' said Sandy, 'because I must see you tonight. Jim's had another disaster!'
> Kath answered, 'Not again! How does he find so much trouble?'

Another way of writing the same piece of text is for you, as a writer, to report what has been said. Here the opening sentence would read:

> Sandy picked up the phone and excitedly asked who was there.

Notice what has happened to the **tense** of the **verb**. It has become past tense. You are reporting what has happened so it must be in the past.

Q Why is reported speech in the past tense?

PRACTICE

Convert the rest of the conversation above into reported speech. Remember, you'll need to change tenses and word order.

Editing your writing

THE BARE BONES

➤ Use time at the end of the exam to improve the quality of your writing.

➤ Focus on extending your vocabulary range as well as improving technical accuracy.

A Writing under exam conditions

1 Always spend a few minutes reading the questions. Make your choice carefully so that you know exactly what type of writing is required.

2 Make a plan before you begin writing.

3 Think about each sentence before you write it.

4 Read your work through as you are writing.

Most students get very bored when told, 'Now check your work!' But it is important to leave time in the exam to do this. Perhaps a more positive instruction is, 'Leave time at the end of the exam to improve the quality of your writing.' This means that you are not just looking at written accuracy but also at things like vocabulary choices in those final few minutes.

Let us look at accuracy first. On many occasions accuracy can be improved, and vital marks gained, by checking for simple errors and slips of the pen. Notice how a little bit of care can make a huge difference to overall accuracy.

Q Re-write this passage to get rid of the common and silly mistakes.

> Sasha could of taken a taxi home but she desided to wait for the bus. The wind was strong it howled down the mane street of broadway. 'Where is the wretched bus she asked herself. it was scary now like the scene in nightmare on elm street.

Editing your writing does not only mean checking the punctuation and spelling. It also means looking at words to see if a more effective choice of vocabulary can be made.

Look at both pieces of writing. Notice how careful checking and editing of vocabulary choices has improved the writing.

> The lites were on as we walked into the town. People were standing around the bars and were making a lot of noice.girls were dressed in brite cloths boys were wearing shorts and t shirts many had tattoos music was coming from inside the bars and you coud here it all over the busy town sqare.

The lights were gleaming as we strolled into town. People were crowding the bars with the noise of their chatter rolling around. Girls displayed garish costumes whilst the boys sported shorts and t shirts; many were adorned with tattoos. Music boomed out from inside the bars and made itself heard around the heaving town square.

There are few, if any, words or punctuation conventions in the changed version which are not well known. It is the effect of editing the writing which has made the difference.

B Vocabulary choices

Now let us look at how some time spent on vocabulary choices can improve the impact on your reader.

Adverbs give more information on the verb. Try to use them especially when the verb is linked to an emotion, e.g. 'She cried despondently at the news' is better than the sentence without the adverb.

Adjectives enhance your description or your ideas. Try to make them precise.

Connectives give variety to your writing. Avoid 'then' and 'so', especially in narrative writing.

Rewrite this passage. Try to improve it, and gain more marks, with imaginative and precise vocabulary choices.

> The mountains looked big as Glen looked up at them. So he went and found his walking boots and rucksack. Then he started to put the nice sandwiches and biscuits in the large bag. He tied up his boots.
> He set out from the house as the rain was starting. It was hitting the windows very hard. He thought about going on such a hard walk. His dad had told him not to although he wanted Glen to act more grown up. Glen always seemed to be in these nasty situations.

Remember
Verbs give movement to a sentence. Make them as dramatic and precise as possible.

PRACTICE

1 Thinking carefully about vocabulary choices, write out a description of one of your favourite teachers.

2 List the adjectives you would use in a description of your favourite method of relaxation.

Comparative questions on 'What Were They Like?' by Denise Levertov and 'Two Scavengers in a Truck' by Lawrence Ferlinghetti

Compare 'What Were They Like?' with 'Two Scavengers in a Truck' to show how the poets reveal their ideas about the cultures they are writing about.

Method

One method is to compare both poems feature by feature. For example, you could start by comparing what the structures of both poems reveal about culture. This could be followed by a comparison of how each poet uses symbolism in relation to culture and so on.

Planning

KEY POINT

1   Look for key words in the question.

The question directs your attention to two specific poems. Some questions ask 'what', which suggests they are concerned with content and subject-matter. This question asks 'how'. A 'how' question requires an answer on the methods used by the poets.

2 Although your answer must compare the methods used, you need to have a clear understanding of what the poems are about. This is so you can say that the poet uses a certain method in order to get a specific message across. You may outline, briefly, at the start of your answer what each poem is about.

Remember
Do not write at length on content – you may become side-tracked.

3 Look for examples of method in both poems. To help your search use this checklist:
* imagery (metaphors, similes, personification, symbolism)
* tone of the language, particularly shifts of tone
* structure (stanzas, different voices, question and answer method)
* rhythm and sound.

Remember
At this stage your ideas will not be fully formed.

4 Read each poem closely. Note, or highlight, features of structure and language. It may help to link features across the poems. This will give you a basis for comparison.
For example:

5 From this plan you can structure an essay (see next page).

Remember
Plan ideas, examples and links.

'What Were They Like?'	'Two Scavengers in a Truck'
set out as question and answer	separate stanzas
numbered points	scruffy scavengers
lantern, bone, ivory	gargoyle Quasimodo
symbols	hip three-piece linen suit
before and after	across that small gulf
charred, bombs, destruction	high seas of democracy
blossom, clouds, moonlight	

Both poets are concerned with society or culture. In 'What Were They Like?' the poet considers the state of a country and its people by showing it at different periods in its history. In 'Two Scavengers in a Truck' the poet explores divisions in a culture, by looking at two different social groups. In the first poem the society is rural, while in the second the picture is of modern urban life.

In the first poem the structure takes the form of question and answer. The effect is that of a pamphlet. The reader may study the information by taking numbered questions and answers together. In this way a picture of before and after hostilities is created. The second poem, however, is structured in clearly defined stanzas. These are used to present the two opposing social groups, the scavengers and the socialites. They are shown, captured together at traffic lights, so that the reader may study them more easily.

The language in the first poem, although set out as a poem, is closer to that of prose: 'Did they use bone and ivory?' 'Who can say?'. The expression sounds rather formal and old-fashioned: 'It is not remembered'. It reflects a society existing in a bygone age. In contrast, Ferlinghetti pictures a society of today, with its 'red, plastic blazers' and 'sunglasses'. The expression for the most part is poetic, though there are prose elements: 'standing on the back stoop'. However, the lines possess a poetic drive with the repetition of the word 'and'.

Both poets use the language of symbolism. In the first poem the symbols of stone, bone and ivory reflect a culture of the countryside. It presents a peaceful atmosphere in tune with 'the opening of buds' and 'quiet laughter'. In the second half of the poem we see the results of warfare through what has happened to these symbols: 'light hearts turned to stone'. Ferlinghetti, however, uses contrasting symbols to separate social groups. The scavengers are 'grungy' from their work and appear like deformed carvings on an old cathedral: 'gargoyle, Quasimodo'. They are filthy and out-of-date. By contrast, the people in the Mercedes are young and in the height of fashion: ' in a hip three-piece linen suit'.

Levertov presents a culture in two halves: one before the war, at peace with itself, the second after the destruction. After the bombs have 'smashed their mirrors', the first half is dimly remembered: 'There is an echo yet'. Ferlinghetti, on the other hand, presents two cultures side by side. They are held together in the traffic 'at the stoplight'. The scavengers gaze down 'at the cool couple'. But they are held together for only a short time: 'an instant' waiting for the light to change. Furthermore, the poet suggests that these two groups will remain separate and distinct, sailing on 'the high seas / of this democracy'. He notes the 'gulf' between them, which suggests the scavengers will always lose out.

Both poets use different methods in order to present pictures of radically different cultures.

Comparative questions on 'Love After Love' by Derek Walcott and 'Half-Caste' by John Agard

Compare the methods the poets use to explore ideas about identity in 'Love After Love' and 'Half-Caste.'

Method

Another method of answering a comparative question is to deal with each poem separately. Write about the first poem, and follow that with a discussion of the second, always making clear points of comparison.

Planning

Remember
Do not expect the examiner to draw the comparisons.

KEY POINT

1   Look for key words in the question.

The question directs your attention to two specific poems. The answer should be about the **methods** used – the 'how'.

2 To answer this question, however, you must also have a clear understanding of the ideas about identity contained in both poems.

3 Remember to consider: language, tone, structure, rhythm and sound.

4 Jot down ideas on identity and highlight examples of method. Link relevant points between the poems.

Remember
Do not write at length on the ideas of identity – summarise them.

Remember
At this stage your ideas will not be fully formed.

'Love After Love'	'Half-Caste'
personal identity/psychological	personal identity, attitudes of others
confident tone – you will	dialect – what yu mean
in Standard English	artistic imagery – Picasso
self versus self – stranger who was yourself	sly dramatic opening – sets tone
rhythm	half-caste – weather, symphony
commands – sit eat	run-on lines, prose
religious imagery	conversational tone
conclusion – left hanging	conclusion – ambiguous

5 From this plan you can structure an essay.

Remember
Plan ideas, examples and links.

th' indicates
s is a
mparative
ay.

e examples of
thod and draw
clusions.

ke clear the
nificance of
agery.

te about your
sonal
ponse.

ers back to the
t poem.

mpare the two
ms and draw
ear distinction.

details to
r meaning.

k for the
ential point.

to end with a
nt of
mparison.

Both poets are concerned with identity. In 'Love After Love' Walcott explores the idea of personal identity by considering the different selves an individual possesses. The emphasis is on a psychological examination of one's personality.

The poem seems to be based on the idea of a counselling session with advice being offered. This raises the question of the identity of the counsellor – priest, psychologist or social worker? Whichever it is, they speak confidently as though they have had plenty of experience of this kind of case: 'The time will come'.

The poem is written in Standard English. The language is quite formal in places: 'whom you ignored' – another indication that the speaker is a professional person. The poem proceeds on a succession of commands: 'Give wine', 'Sit'. This indicates that the person speaks with a good deal of authority.

The subject of the poem is continually being asked to face up to other aspects of themselves. The other selves are pictured arriving at the house ('At your own door') or appearing in the mirror. They can be found in the content of 'love letters', or pictured in 'photographs' and 'desperate notes'. These might suggest the person is coming out of a relationship. It is not a comfortable time. There is an air of anxiety about this meeting with the person's other selves.

There is a religious tone to the verse. Commands associated with the services of mass or communion are given: 'Give wine. Give bread.' The conclusion continues the theme: 'Feast on your life.' Through this imagery, comfort and support are offered. Although warm and helpful in tone, the conclusion leaves the reader feeling uncertain. Is the eating to be seen as a religious act of 'eating' the body of Christ as in the mass or communion? Could the 'feast' be suggesting the need for celebration of a person's life?

In 'Half-Caste' the poet also tackles the problem of personal identity. The subject is of mixed race, a 'half-caste' person. The poem shows that the problem lies not with the man but with those who are prejudiced against him.

In contrast with the measured tone of 'Love After Love', Agard buttonholes the reader. He addresses the reader directly in a dramatic fashion: 'Excuse me / standing on one leg.' He challenges the reader: 'Explain yuself'. The reader is asked to define his position: 'what yu mean / when yu say half-caste.'

For much of the poem he speaks in a West Indian dialect – 'what yu mean' – though, like Walcott, he does use Standard English : 'consequently when I dream'. The difference here is that he is showing that by being fluent in both languages he is equally at home in two cultures. Agard mocks the attitude of people who see him as incomplete: 'cast half a shadow'. He uses western cultural symbols (Tchaikovsky and Picasso) to uncover the prejudice in people. These are the people, he seems to be suggesting, who would reduce classical music to a collection of black and white notes. These are the same people who see others only in terms of their colour.

The imagery drawn from the arts contrasts with the religious imagery of the first poem. Agard's purpose is to strengthen his attack on prejudice, whereas Walcott emphasises the healing powers of religion. As in 'Love After Love' the conclusion of 'Half-Caste' leaves the reader in the air. This is not because it is ambiguous, but because the poet is saving part of his story for when the listener is fully aware, 'wid de whole of yu eye', of what prejudice means.

Comparative questions on 'Presents from my Aunts in Pakistan' by Moniza Alvi and 'Night of the Scorpion' by Nissim Ezekiel

Compare the ways poets present people in 'Presents from my Aunts in Pakistan' and 'Night of the Scorpion'.

Method

In this example the method used is that of comparing paired features to be found in both poems.

Planning

1 This is basically a 'how' question, so the preparation mainly focuses on the poetic methods used.

2 In order to anchor your arguments, briefly indicate the various types of people who are the subjects of the poems.

3 Remember to consider: language, tone, structure, rhythm and sound.

4 Note/highlight examples of method. Link relevant points between the poems.

'Presents from my Aunts in Pakistan'	'Night of the Scorpion'
the persona, the aunts, men and women	mother, father, peasants, poet
persona caught between two cultures	persona observer of events
aunts in traditional culture	people showing cultural attitudes
symbols of dress and jewellery	behaviour and speech of different groups
colour associated with dress	effect of speech and behaviour on poet
effect of wearing different dress	social groups seen together
references back to Pakistani society	poetry continuous apart from conclusion
stanzas, long lines and short	different tone for each group
short phrases and their effect	

5 From this plan you can structure an essay.

Remember
Do not write at length about the subjects of the poems – summarise.

Remember
At this stage your ideas will not be fully formed.

Remember
Plan ideas, examples and links.

In 'Presents from my Aunts in Pakistan' the poet examines the effect of cultural change. The change is seen through the eyes of a person who has left a traditional society and is contemplating her life in a western culture. She explores the conflict she feels because of this change. In so doing, she comments on the people still bound to a traditional way of life: her aunts of the title. The writer of 'Night of the Scorpion' also contemplates cultural differences, but he pictures cultural groups gathered together in one place. He observes different reactions to a single event: his mother bitten by a scorpion. The 'actors' in this drama are his mother, his father and a group of peasants. His own attitude is to be gathered from the way he describes the scene.

Moniza Alvi indicates a person's cultural position through the symbolism of dress and personal ornament. The persona first appears in traditional costume: 'embossed slippers, gold and black', 'Candy-striped glass bangles', some of the presents from her aunts, who still live in Pakistan. She finds their type of dress an 'alien' feature in her sitting room. Moreover, the costume is felt to be threatening. The bangles 'snapped, drew blood'. Her preference is for western clothing: 'denim and corduroy'. She may even feel ashamed of her traditional costume. She notes that they are 'radiant'; nevertheless, she keeps them in her wardrobe.

By contrast, Ezekiel represents cultural differences through the behaviour and speech of the participants in the little drama. The peasants are shown to be irritating, by the poet comparing them to 'a swarm of flies'. The persona's contempt for their practices is shown when they 'buzzed' the name of God. Their candles threw threatening shadows onto the walls: 'giant scorpion shadows'. The clicking of their tongues, he found annoying. Their formal protestations to God – 'may the sum of evil / balanced in the unreal world / against the sum of good' – make them sound long-winded and pretentious. The poet heightens this feeling of irritation by repeating the word 'more': 'More candles, more lanterns, more neighbours'. The fact that the father is supposed to be a 'sceptic' adds emphasis to the desperation of his actions when he sets fire to his wife's bitten toe. This is captured by the persona in the word 'even' in line 39.

The first poet comments on cultural differences by allowing her persona to reflect on her own background. She 'pictured her birthplace'. She could see her aunts experiencing a very different lifestyle: 'in shaded rooms / shaded from male visitors'. She imagines that she has lost her cultural identity as she stares 'at the Shalimar gardens'. The 'fretwork' is the barrier which separates her from her past. It allows her to see what is happening in a different society, but it refuses her entry. The participants in 'Night of the Scorpion', although appearing together, are separated by their speech and behaviour. The poet finds 'the peace of understanding on each face' a kind of barrier to understanding the peasants.

The verse pattern in 'Presents from my Aunts in Pakistan' consists of stanzas containing long and short lines. The long lines are descriptive either of dress or memories. They are rich in colour and detail – 'glistening like an orange split open' – to create a vivid picture of a traditional society. The short lines are used to focus on significant points: 'playing with a tin boat' emphasises the girl's loneliness. On the other hand, 'Night of the Scorpion' is written in continuous verse, which often has the feeling of prose. For example, 'I remember the night my mother…' reads like the opening of a factual account. There is variety of expression, however, with the incantations of the peasants and the heartfelt 'Thank God' of the poet's mother.

Both poets use similar techniques of tone shifts and symbolism. They do, however, differ in the overall framework (poetic description of a culture, as opposed to prosaic account of a dramatic event). The one uses a time gap to emphasise a gap between peoples and cultures: the other uses a child's perceptions to point out the ridiculous in the way people behave.

Margin annotations:

- ...mpare content, ...icating ...ilarities and ...erences.
- ...arly identify ...thod.
- ...w the ...nificance of the ...mbolism.
- ...v contrast
- ...alify the ...aning of ...rds.
- ...velop ...mments using ...dence from the ...
- ...w how the ...t achieves an ...ct.
- ...er to similar ...mbols in the ...ms.
- ...ays make ...r the ...nificance of an ...ge.
- ...fly summarise ... differences.

Non-fiction and media texts

Reading

How do the choices of form, layout and presentation contribute to the effect of the language in this media text?

Comment on:

- what the advertisement contains

- how the material is presented

- the language it uses.

One of these tomatoes is contaminated by E.coli

(If you can't tell which, don't worry.)

Food poisoning is on the increase.

E.coli bacteria have now been found not just on meat, but on the surface of fruit and vegetables too. (They'd been fertilised with contaminated manure.)

To make matters worse, certain types of E.coli have even developed a resistance to some antibiotics.

Isn't anything safe to eat any more?

The good news is, E.coli bacteria have a deadly enemy: Milton Fluid.

In fact Milton, when diluted with water and used as recommended, kills all germs.

No wonder more and more people are buying it, whether there's a baby in the house or not.

And they're using it not just on their fridges, kitchen surfaces and chopping boards, but also for rinsing fruit and salad vegetables.

Perhaps doing that sounds a bit odd, eccentric even.

If it does, why not try this test for yourself: following the instructions on the pack, rinse some tomatoes, grapes or other fruit in diluted Milton, then let them drain until the surface is completely dry.

When you come to eat them, you'll find that Milton hasn't even changed the taste at all. (Even though it will have killed germs by the million.)

Better still, fruit and veg rinsed in Milton stay fresh for days longer.

That's because Milton kills the bacteria that make food go off, as well as the ones that cause food poisoning.

Maybe it's not such an odd thing to do after all. More like common sense, in fact.

Especially when the alternative is just hoping for the best.

FAMILY PROTECTION FROM FOOD GERMS

Answering this type of question

A   What skills do I need?

You are expected to:

1   write about the contents of the text, showing that you have followed and understood the writer's argument

2   comment on presentational devices such as headlines, illustrations, different types of font. You should also comment on the link between the headline, illustration and printed text.

3   identify the purpose of the text and show how the writer uses language to achieve this purpose

4   explain how readers might respond to the text, giving clear reasons.

B Extra tips

To do well when answering questions on reading non-fiction, you should follow these steps:

1 Read the question first and then skim-read the text.

2 Underline the key words in the question and then scan the text for details that you will need to answer the question.

3 Remember to refer closely to the text, using either quotations or your own words.

4 Always include references to the purpose and audience of a text.

C Remember:

1 Follow the bullet-points closely – they are your guide to writing exactly what the examiner expects.

2 This question carries the highest number of marks, so make sure you answer in detail.

Model answer

Includes reference to key word in question.

Comments on language in early part of answer.

Quotation used to support point.

Able to analyse the effect of presentational devices.

Pays attention to the details of the text.

Shows understanding of layout in the advertisement.

The first paragraph contains information about food-poisoning bacteria. The scientific name is used, which convinces readers that this is a serious article. The main part of the article tells readers about how Milton Fluid can be used to destroy bacteria. The writers have used this information to give readers advice about safe food preparation. The article persuades readers to buy Milton Fluid by convincing them that it kills all germs. It uses the phrase 'common sense', which makes the reader think that using Milton Fluid is a very good idea.

The presentation is eye-catching. The bold headline 'One of these tomatoes is contaminated by E.coli' is an effective way to catch the reader's attention because 'contaminated' is such a dramatic word. This heading is also written in a different font from the main text, which serves to catch the reader's eye. The small caption at the bottom of the advertisement – 'family protection from food germs' – is a reminder of the advertisement's purpose to persuade readers that Milton Fluid is safe and therefore that they should buy it.

There is a lot of writing in the advert, which might put some readers off, but the paragraphs are short, which will make reading easier and so encourage readers to take in the message. The advertisement persuades readers by using an informal tone; it sounds as if someone is talking directly to them. For example, 'If you can't tell which, don't worry.' The use of the word 'you' appeals directly to the reader, as does the use of the question, 'Isn't anything safe to eat any more?'

Able to summarise argument.

Addresses focus of question.

Shows clear awareness of purpose of text.

Analyses language and its effect on the reader.

Non-fiction and media texts

Writing

Use this information about bullying to help you write an advice sheet for parents on how to cope if their child is a bully or is being bullied.

The Balance of Playground Power

- One in five children in Britain is either a bully or a victim of bullying. Some researchers believe this is just the tip of the iceberg: they think more like 70 per cent of the school population is involved.

- A pilot study of 4,000 primary schoolchildren for Kidscape, the children's safety group, revealed that 38 per cent had been bullied, and that bullying was one of children's main worries.

- Male bullies outnumber female bullies three to one. Boys bully both sexes, girls generally tend to stick to their own sex.

- There is a higher incidence of bullying in urban schools than in rural schools.

- Statistics say 68 per cent of all school bullies will become violent adults. A bully has a 25 per cent chance of committing crime in adult life (the average is five per cent).

- Strong links have been established between truancy, underachievement and bullying.

Answering this type of question

A What skills do I need?

You are expected to:

1 match the style of your writing to your audience and purpose – in this case the **audience** is **adults** and the **purpose** is to **advise**

2 organise your ideas so that your readers can easily follow your ideas

3 use some presentational devices to attract and hold the attention of your audience.

B Extra tips

To do well in writing non-fiction texts in examination conditions, you should follow these steps:

1 Plan your ideas and the order in which you will write them.

2 Choose your words carefully and aim to use a wide range of vocabulary.

C Remember:

1 Check your work for mistakes as you are writing – check after every paragraph, as it is easier to correct mistakes at this stage.

2 Read through your work when it is finished, to check for spelling and punctuation mistakes.

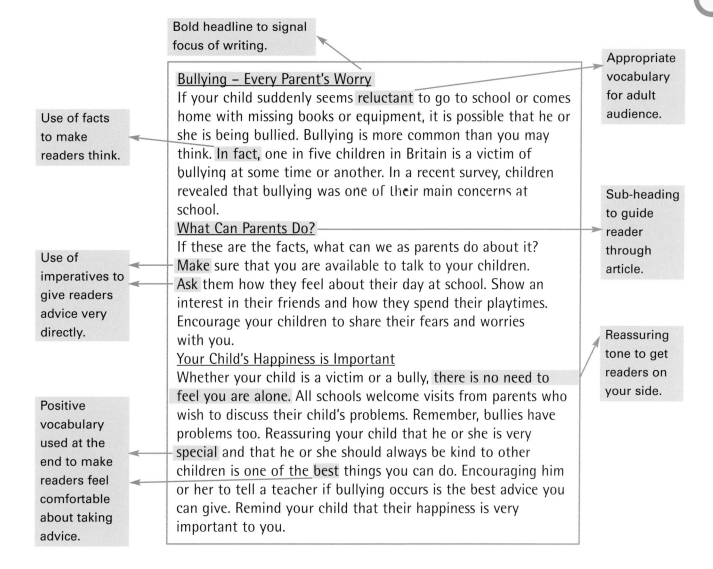

Bold headline to signal focus of writing.

Appropriate vocabulary for adult audience.

Use of facts to make readers think.

Sub-heading to guide reader through article.

Use of imperatives to give readers advice very directly.

Reassuring tone to get readers on your side.

Positive vocabulary used at the end to make readers feel comfortable about taking advice.

Bullying – Every Parent's Worry

If your child suddenly seems reluctant to go to school or comes home with missing books or equipment, it is possible that he or she is being bullied. Bullying is more common than you may think. In fact, one in five children in Britain is a victim of bullying at some time or another. In a recent survey, children revealed that bullying was one of their main concerns at school.

What Can Parents Do?

If these are the facts, what can we as parents do about it? Make sure that you are available to talk to your children. Ask them how they feel about their day at school. Show an interest in their friends and how they spend their playtimes. Encourage your children to share their fears and worries with you.

Your Child's Happiness is Important

Whether your child is a victim or a bully, there is no need to feel you are alone. All schools welcome visits from parents who wish to discuss their child's problems. Remember, bullies have problems too. Reassuring your child that he or she is very special and that he or she should always be kind to other children is one of the best things you can do. Encouraging him or her to tell a teacher if bullying occurs is the best advice you can give. Remind your child that their happiness is very important to you.

Other writing questions you will find in examinations

- You could also be asked to write to persuade.

For example:

Write a letter to your headteacher persuading him or her to improve facilities for Year 11 students in your school.

- You could be asked to write to argue.

For example:

Write an article for a magazine read by parents in which you argue the case for the abolition of homework.

Cluster One poems

'Two Scavengers in a Truck, Two Beautiful People in a Mercedes' by Lawrence Ferlinghetti

Complete this chart.

Phrase	What it suggests about character
Hip three-piece linen suit	
Casually coiffed	
Grungy from their route	
Gargoyle Quasimodo	

Now use your suggestions to write a paragraph on the contrast between the two sets of people in the poem.

'Vultures' by Chinua Achebe

Complete this chart

Image from the poem	Picture you get of the vulture
Cold telescopic eyes	
A pebble on a stem	
Nestled close to his mate	
A dump of gross feathers	

Now use your ideas to write a paragraph comparing these aspects of the vulture to the Belsen Commandant.

'Blessings' by Imtiaz Dharker

Make a list of references in the poem to religious worship and valuable possessions.

Write a paragraph explaining why you think the writer has used these references.

'Limbo' by Edward Kamau Brathwaite

This poem reflects the dreadful conditions in which slaves were transported from Africa. The journey on the ship was like the limbo dance. Complete this chart.

Part of limbo dance	Part of journey
Very bottom of dance	
Start to rise up	
Fully stand upright	

Cluster Two poems

'Unrelated Incidents' by Tom Leonard
Complete this chart:

Phrase	Suggests about the speaker's attitude to his audience
Thi reason/a talk wia/BBC accent	
Lik wanna yoo/scruff	
this/is ma trooth	
Yi canny talk/right	

'Half-Caste' by John Agard
Complete this chart:

Symbols of half-caste culture	Contains the two halves of...
Picasso	
Half-caste weather	
England weather	
Tchaikovsky	

'Presents from my Aunts in Pakistan' by Moniza Alvi

Fill in the gaps from this piece on 'Presents from my Aunts in Pakistan' with words or phrases from the poem:

> The poet pictures two separate cultures through symbols of clothing. In the first stanza, she uses such descriptions as _____ to create a society of beauty. However, some fashions give a feeling of discomfort, as in _____ , as though the poet feels she does not quite belong in this society. She prefers western clothing, as in her reference to _____ . She feels slightly embarrassed about fashions from her country of origin. She keeps her presents in her _____ .

'Not my Business' by Niyi Osundare
Complete this chart:

Lines from poem	What has happened and how the writer feels about it
They picked Akanni up one morning	
Beat him like soft clay	
They came one night	
Booted the whole house awake	
Chinwe went to work one day	
Only to find her job was gone	

Now write a paragraph where you compare the writer's attitude to one of these events to what happened to the writer in stanza four.

Non-fiction and media texts

Reading

1 Which of the following texts are non-fiction or media texts?

newspaper article	advertisement	poem	script of radio broadcast
short story	web page	information leaflet	travel brochure
extract from autobiography	scene of a play	novel	travel writing

2 List the facts and opinions in the following passage:

> The school has approximately 1,325 pupils. Many of these pupils live within a two mile radius of the school and could easily walk there. Two school buses transport children from outside the catchment area. The school seems to be very popular with parents although, in appearance, it is not particularly attractive. It was built in the sixties and the large glass windows must be a nightmare in the summer when the sun is shining.

3 Read the letter on the next page. Identify:

- the intended purpose and audience
- the key point in each paragraph.

3 Eastern Approach
Waterton
West Mendip
BJ37 6GB

31st March 2004

The Editor
The Daily Look
23 Lyme Harbour
London
EC14 7WX

Dear Editor,

My daughter's school is set in the middle of a large urban area. Most of the pupils who attend it live less than one mile away. Yet, every morning, the approach to the school is blocked because parents, in their hundreds, are dropping off their children. A short walk, that would do most of these kids a world of good, is replaced by a lazy ride in a gas-guzzling machine.

We all know that lack of fitness and obesity in the young are growing problems. Here is an ideal chance to increase the daily exercise routine of the average young person. Let's stop this over-protective madness. Make the children walk. Put their health first and at the same time make our roads safer and reduce unnecessary pollution.

Yours sincerely,

K. Watson

4 List five different presentational features which might appear in a media text.

5 Read the following passage. Identify the different methods the writer uses to get her point across to the reader.

Have you ever dreamt of lying on a sun-soaked beach, sipping cocktails and listening to the gentle sounds of the waves as they rush onto the sand? Well, it could become more than a dream. All you have to do to make this dream become a reality is complete the form below. Send us your name, postal and e-mail address and we'll make sure your name is entered in our 'Dream of a lifetime' competition. What could be easier?

Writing

1 How would the style of your writing be different if you were:

- writing for a young child
- writing to an MP (Member of Parliament)
- writing to your best friend?

Identify precisely the different features of the writing.

2 Devise a plan for the following exam question. Remember your plan needs to show a range of ideas and the order in which you will write about them. Start by highlighting the key words in the question.

> Write a letter to a relative who lives in another country and whom you have not seen for some time. Inform him or her of the things that have been happening to you and your family over recent months.

3 List the ideas you would use to argue that more should be done to clear up litter either in your school or in your home area. Think about what arguments could be made against you, e.g. the cost, and how you would counter these.

4 Write the 50-word text for an advertisement for a new chocolate bar called 'Maxi', or something else.

Your aim is to persuade readers to try it. Highlight the words you have used that are designed to persuade.

5 Underline the adjectives and verbs in the following passage. Change and/or add to these with words which demonstrate a 'sophisticated vocabulary range' and which create a more effective description:

The playground was filled with students. There were the noisy first year boys playing silly games in one corner and trying to tease the Year nine girls. In another corner the smokers were standing together in a circle fooling themselves that no-one knew what they were doing. Behind the temporary classroom one girl stood on her own, avoiding the playground bullies. The teachers patrolled the playground, keeping tight hold of their mugs of coffee and occasionally chatting to a group of students.

This glossary provides a quick and handy reference to some of the terms used in this book. Use it to check you understand the words and that you can use them correctly in your own answers.

Alliteration

repeating consonants that sound the same at the beginning of words or stressed syllables. *Example: sound of blue surf.*

Argument

the meaning a writer wants to convey in a piece of writing.

Assonance

giving the impression that words sound similar by repeating the same or similar vowel sounds. *Example: sun surfacing.*

Brainstorming

writing down all the various possible meanings and interpretations you can think of after reading a particular piece of writing, for example.

Colloquialism

an informal word, phrase or piece of English you might use when chatting. *Example: 'hip' instead of 'up-to-date'.*

Context

the text which surrounds a word or phrase. A word may fit into its context or may appear to surprise you and be out of context.

Cross-referencing

reading or writing about the different works of an author or authors to point out similarities in content and/or types of expression.

Culture

a person's culture is to be found in an accumulation of various influences, which may include: social, educational, political and religious. It is important to remember that place of birth and language have a significant bearing on a person's culture, too. Poets in this selection are interested in the effect of the cultural influences on a person's life.

Dialogue

conversation between characters.

Emotive language

words or phrases that arouse an emotional response in the reader. *Example: Hands burn for a stone.*

Figure of speech

where the meaning of a particular expression isn't the same as the literal meaning of the words. *Example: She was over the moon.*

Imagery/images

is the general term to cover figures of speech (metaphor, simile, etc.). Through the use of imagery a writer projects different images to the reader/listener.

Irony

using language to express the opposite to what you mean or feel.

Metaphor

describing something by saying it is another thing. *Example: he's a wizard at maths. (See also Simile.)*

Narrative method/style

how the author tells a story in a piece of writing.

Persona

poets often write in the first person. Remember that the person speaking to you in the poem is not necessarily the voice of the poet. The poet is using a device, a persona, to raise important issues and express different attitudes. Notice the use of persona in 'Limbo' and 'Nothing's Changed'.

Personification

giving things or ideas human characteristics. *Example: The Jeep was waiting.*

Prose

a form of writing that is not in verse and that doesn't rhyme. Novels and newspapers are written in prose.

Received pronunciation

this accent is used by speakers of Standard English who do not possess a regional accent.

Rhyme

using pairs or groups of words, usually at the end of lines of verse, which have the same or very similar sounds.

Rhyme scheme

used to discuss the way a poem rhymes. Write 'A' to denote the sound of the last word of the first line. If the second line ends with the same sound, write 'A' again. If it's different, write 'B'. Do the same thing with all the lines in the poem. You might find that the rhyme scheme of a poem with three four-line stanzas is AABB, or ABAB, or ABCA, etc.

Rhyming couplet

two consecutive lines of verse that rhyme with each other, and are usually about the same length. If the rhyme scheme of a poem is AABBCC and so on, the poem is written in rhyming couplets.

Rhythm

a term usually applied to poetry, but which can also be used for drama and prose. Rhythm is produced by the stress given to words when they are read aloud. If the stress falls on words at regular intervals, this is called regular rhythm. If the stress falls with no particular pattern, this is called irregular rhythm.

Simile

describing something by saying it is *'like'* or *'as'* something else. *Example: glistening like an orange split open. (See also Metaphor.)*

Standard English

as the name suggests, this is the form of written English which is commonly accepted as the norm in aspects of grammar, syntax and spelling.

Stanza

a poem is usually divided into lines grouped together called stanzas. In hymn-books they are called verses, but make sure you use the word *stanza* in poetry.

Symbol

a word that stands for an object and what it represents. Many poets use their own personal symbols. John Agard uses Picasso as a symbol of western culture.

Texture

the pattern of rhythm and sound in a poem. A piece of material has a texture built up by the threads used to make it and the way it is woven. Poetry has a texture too, made by the words used and the way they are used.

Transferred epithet

examples of this feature an adjective (epithet) which has been moved (transferred) from one person or thing to another. *Example: bewildered lawn.*

Verse

a term applied to poetic writing, not prose. Note that a verse (singular) is a single line of a poem.

Word association

using words whose meaning can be used to suggest another meaning. The word *red*, for example, means a colour, but it can also suggest danger or a political belief.

Poetry

'Vultures' by Chinua Achebe
- Compares scavengers with the Commandant of Belsen.
- Vultures' habits seem unpleasant – the Commandant is evil.
- Poet finds humour in the vultures' domestic life.
- Commandant appearing as dutiful father is hypocritical.
- Verse set out in unrhymed lines.
- Lines run on like a paragraph of prose.

'Nothing's Changed' by Tatamkhulu Afrika
- Clash of two cultures.
- Persona feels at one with the natural world.
- To him nature is favourable – 'amiable weeds'.
- New development excludes local people.
- Symbol of glass acts as barrier.
- Desire to rebel – stone, bomb.
- Ambiguous conclusion.

'Half-Caste' by John Agard
- Persona happy with his cultural situation.
- Confident in either Caribbean or western culture.
- Mocks the critics of the half-caste man.
- Attacks their ludicrous position by comparing it to half-caste weather.
- Ridicules cultural beliefs of those who see classical music in black and white terms.
- Their racial prejudices are revealed through half-formed ideas.
- Dramatic, colloquial style.

'Presents from my Aunts in Pakistan' by Moniza Alvi
- Cultural differences between Pakistan and the United Kingdom.
- Cultural differences between the young and the elderly.
- Culture expressed in the symbols of clothing and decoration.
- Images of discomfort reveal person caught between two cultures.
- Traditional culture expressed through out-of-date practices.
- Isolated phrases increase sense of loneliness.

'Search For My Tongue' by Sujata Bhatt
- Cultural identity seen as language.
- Language expressed through physical tongues.
- Original language has died in the mouth.
- New tongue grows from a stump in the mouth.
- Extended image of a growing tongue culminates in 'blossoms'.
- Phonetic lines of Gujarati enable reader to understand her tongue.

'Limbo' by Edward Kamau Brathwaite
- Poetic rhythm re-creates the movement of the limbo dancer.
- Compares the dance with life on a slave ship.
- Symbol of 'stick' used to link the dance with slavery.
- 'Dark' is seen as both night and the evil of slavery.
- Poet feels the presence of gods in the music.
- The music saves the dancer from evil/former life of a slave.

'Blessing' and 'This Room' by Imtiaz Dharker
- Poems open dramatically.
- Objects possess a life of their own.
- Poet conveys meaning through sound.
- Alliteration gives the writing vitality.
- Each poem is written as a lively crescendo.
- Climax may be positive or disturbing, as an anti-climax.

'Night of the Scorpion' by Nissim Ezekiel
- Structured around the reactions of different people.
- The peasants shown to be superstitious.
- Father is sceptical.
- Mother is a stoic and thinks only of her children.
- More poetic style used to describe the peasants' reactions.
- Father is described in a prosaic, matter-of-fact way.

'Two Scavengers in a Truck' by Lawrence Ferlinghetti
- Two distinct cultural groups.
- Scavengers presented through symbols of dirt and deformity.
- Socialites described as clean and fashionable.
- Groups arrive together at a set of traffic lights.
- Verse used to bring them together in stanzas.
- Both belong to same democracy but are separated by a gulf.

'Unrelated Incidents' by Tom Leonard
- Based on a language culture clash.
- Compares the relative standing of Standard English and dialects.
- Place in society determined by the way one speaks.
- Comic effect of BBC newsreader speaking Glaswegian.
- Poem questions acceptability of regional accents in the media.
- Poem questions the authority of those who speak RP.

'What Were They Like?' by Denise Levertov
- Poem presented like a pamphlet.
- Set of numbered questions and answers.
- Set out as poem but reads in places like prose.
- Symbols of peace in the questions.

- The answers reveal what has happened to them.
- Some expressions are dated to represent a society not accustomed to modern ways.

'Hurricane Hits England' and 'Island Man' by Grace Nichols

- Concerned with two contrasting cultures.
- Cultures linked through nature (sea and hurricane).
- Close relationship between person and nature.
- Imaginative/experimental use of language.
- Word association often ensures a link between cultures.
- Produces new ways of looking at things.

'Not My Business' by Niyi Osundare

- Examples of citizens arrested by the state.
- Chorus attached to stanzas, with the exception of the last.
- Eating the yam is the symbol of the persona's indifference.
- Violence of many arrests.
- Persona seems detached from events/politics/society.
- Transferred epithet (bewildered lawn) stresses air of detachment.

'Love After Love' by Derek Walcott

- Questions of personal identity.
- Subject is being advised (by psychiatrist, social worker, priest?).
- Adviser shows understanding of this question and its solution.
- Different selves meet at the door/in the mirror.
- Religious imagery suggests a possible way forward.
- Ends on note of celebration.

Reading Non-fiction and Media Texts

- Read the questions first, then read the texts.
- Use skimming and scanning techniques to help you find answers.
- Underline or highlight key parts of the texts.
- Refer to the texts frequently to support your answers. Do not copy from the text unless the question asks you to.
- Facts can be proved to be true. Opinions cannot be proved to be true.
- When following an argument, aim to identify the key points in each paragraph.
- The purpose is the reason for which something is designed and written.
- The audience is the intended reader or viewer.
- Use clues in presentation and content to help you identify intended purpose and audience.
- Presentational features include: bold print, underlining, variety of fonts, photographs and illustrations, headlines and sub-headings, logos.
- Writers might address the reader directly, use rhetorical questions, imperatives, alliteration, puns, exaggeration, emotive language and colloquial language to draw attention to a particular point.
- When comparing texts writers think about: purpose and audience, content, structure, presentation and use of language.

Writing

- You need to vary the style of your writing depending on your purpose and audience. For example, when writing for young children you would use simple vocabulary, simple sentence structures and frequent repetition of ideas. When writing to a friend you might use informal language, questions, exclamations and ellipses. When writing to an MP (Member of Parliament) you would use Standard English, adopt a formal tone, use a range of simple, compound and complex sentences and sophisticated vocabulary. You might still use rhetorical questions and exclamations for effect.
- Always plan before starting to write. Aim to identify purpose and audience, to get a range of ideas together and to decide on the order in which you are going to write them. Remember the plan is for *your* benefit and will improve your final piece of writing.
- When writing to argue make your points clearly and consider points that could be made against you. Useful phrases to remember are: 'It could be argued that...', 'However...', 'On the other hand ...'.
- When writing to persuade, you are trying to get your readers to do something. You could address the reader directly, use emotive language to appeal to their feelings and use exaggeration to make something sound better than it is.
- When writing to advise, you need to show you understand your reader's feelings and reassure him or her about their difficulties. Your advice is more likely to be effective if you use the word 'could' instead of 'should'.
- When writing to inform, you need to include a range of relevant detail. You should include facts and opinions. Remember that in an exam you can make the 'facts' up.
- When writing to explain you are answering the questions 'How?' and 'Why?' An explanation gives reasons for something. When planning, use these two words as a starting-point for ideas.
- When writing to describe, you are trying to create a picture for your reader. You need to make very careful choices of words in order to make that picture as effective as possible.
- It is important that you ensure your writing is as technically accurate as possible. Make sure you correct common spelling errors and that you read through your work every ten minutes to ensure it communicates your ideas clearly. A range of punctuation is essential to help your reader make sense of what you have written.

Note that answers are given only to those questions which have specific answers. The more open-ended questions demanding extended answers should be checked by someone with understanding of the subject.

Page 8　Margin 1
The difficulty of the dance mirrors the struggle the speaker of the poem had in crossing from one culture to another. The stick is a symbol of punishment – slaves were beaten. The stick is a barrier for the dancer. He or she must struggle to overcome social and class barriers in their new country.

Margin 3
In mediaeval times the church taught that when we die our souls first visit a place called Limbo. This place is neither Heaven nor Hell. It was thought to be a waiting room for souls until God decided which were destined for Heaven and which were going to Hell. It has come to mean a place where you hang about waiting for something to happen. In the poem, while the dancer is moving slowly under the stick he or she is in a kind of limbo. Similarly, the immigrants sailing across the Atlantic are caught between two types of existence.

Margin 4
The word 'dark' suggests a dangerous journey, on which unpleasant things happen. They remain a secret to the rest of the world who cannot see what terrible things are happening in the darkness below decks.

Page 9　Margin 2
The word 'half' symbolises the speaker's problem. He is looked upon by the rest of society as half belonging to a West Indian culture and half belonging to a white European culture. He, like the limbo dancer, is caught between two existences. He expresses his feelings about his situation by writing about examples of life seen as two halves. In this way he shows how stupid people are to see him as only half a man.

Page 10　Margin 1
The word 'another' could suggest another lover who has taken the place of the person's real self.

Margin 2
People write love letters which are 'desperate' because they feel so much in love and are 'desperate' to express their love. On the other hand, they might fear that they are losing their loved one and are 'desperate' to keep the relationship going.

Page 11　Margin 1
Ministers of all religions, psychiatrists, social workers, teachers, parents, friends.

Margin 2
As Jesus invited his followers to feast on himself in the form of the bread and the wine, so we can feast on ourselves. We do not literally eat ourselves, but celebrate our existence and our worth when we eat and drink.

Practice 1
The use of instructions indicates clear remedies. The tone suggests that the advice giver is speaking from experience and possesses authority. This confident tone increases a feeling of confidence in the recipient. The instructions, however, do not admit questions, and there seem to be some important questions which require answers.

Page 13　Practice 2
The repetition fixes key impressions in the reader's mind: the scavengers are physically superior to the smart young people, though actually socially inferior; the fashionable eye-wear stresses their fashion-consciousness; the light emphasises the fact that both sets of people have been drawn together, as signalled by the traffic lights.

Page 16　Margin 2
The speaker of the poem is deadly serious about the value of his native accent and dialect. The preservation of individual speech, he sees, is vitally important to the preservation of our identity. If we all spoke the same, would we become just like everybody else?

Margin 3
A newscaster with a regional accent may make many of the listeners feel comfortable, hearing a friendly voice. The broadcaster is not seen as an outsider who might appear to be uninterested in local issues.

Page 18　Margin 1
The word 'perform' suggests the holy man is acting out a part. As an actor is aware of his audience, so the speaker is suggesting this man is conscious of the people in the room, and therefore may be more interested in them than in doing some good.

Margin 2
The separation serves to emphasise his mother's words. They sound genuine, unlike many of the actions of people in the room.

Page 19　Margin 1
The people are described as 'odorless' as a TV ad, since you cannot smell performers on TV. Because of this they may seem unreal to the viewers. Similarly, the couple are described as 'odorless' because they seem unreal to the smelly scavengers.

Page 20　Margin 1
Colour is used to indicate differences between two cultures. The society which the Aunts inhabit is usually described in vivid colours, whereas western culture is denoted by subdued tones. The preference of the speaker is for the quieter colours of denim and corduroy.

Margin 2
The speaker indicates that her parents have adopted western society by the subdued colour of their 'camel-skin lamp'. It is interesting to note that she is using the lamp to examine the bright colours of the country where she was born.

Margin 3
Both phrases indicate separation: the first by concealing them in tissue so that they cannot be seen; the second phrase shows a physical barrier which separates the women from the men, though the women are permitted to look through gaps in the 'fretwork'.

Page 21　Margin 1
By repeating the word 'earth' the speaker is emphasising the value of the earth. She may be suggesting that there is nothing in the universe that can be compared with it. Note two meanings of this word. It can mean both the stuff on which man walks and the planet which man inhabits. As the substance, earth can symbolise our existence and the place to which many are returned after death.

Page 22　Margin 1
A womb which is full of child is round like a huge breaker. The wave bursts and loses its roundness, just as a woman's shape flattens after giving birth.

Margin 2
The word 'defiantly' emphasises the suddenness of sunrise, in the same way as a defiant person might suddenly shout or wave a fist at you. There is a suggestion of rebellion in the word, which might indicate a struggle between man and nature.

Page 23　Margin 1
Besides describing the size of the children, the word 'small' could indicate that their growth has been stunted through undernourishment. The reader is invited to sympathise with their plight through the emotive use of 'small'.
'The steady breaking and wombing' could suggest an inevitable tide which is teaming with life.
'grey metallic soar' Where the reader might expect the 'roar' of the traffic, the poet writes 'soar'. This little device may indicate that the

noise of traffic is increasing. Applied to the man, it could suggest his thoughts are soaring above the traffic.

'to surge of wheels' the surge of the sea becomes, or becomes confused with, the traffic surge.

'his crumpled pillow waves' Again the poet links the man's London experience with life back on the island. His pillow is 'crumpled', suggesting disturbed sleep. The shape of the pillow brings to his mind the waves on his native shore.

Page 24 Margin 2
The word 'rebelliously' shows that the Commandant would prefer to forget that his job is the extermination of Jews, but the smell of burnt flesh clings to him. It is described as rebelling, because it is a constant reminder to the Commandant.

Page 25 Margin 1
The word 'germ' can mean a seed which brings life (the germ of an idea) or it can be a means of spreading disease. The 'germ' of the Commandant could bring life, but instead it produces death.

Margin 2
Her new tongue grows and flourishes in her mouth like a tree in a full flower. It becomes fully developed and a thing of great beauty.

Page 27 Margin 1
'flaring' means showy , gaudy and suggests that the flag does not fit in with the quiet lifestyle of locals.

'guard' suggests that the development requires protection from the people who live locally, as though they are a threat.

'crushed' means that the ice has been carefully prepared. In context, the word 'crushed' becomes associated with the local people who have had their hopes crushed.

Margin 2
'I back from the glass' shows that the man feels repulsed by the new development.

'shiver down the glass' – the word 'shiver' means to break, shatter, which is what the man hopes will happen to the new glass. By association the word could describe the man's reaction to the glass. He shivers or trembles with rage.

Page 28 Margin 1
The description makes the sacking sound frightening, because Chinwe was a model worker. If such a person can be sacked so quickly, what hope is there for all the other workers?

Margin 2
'Waiting, waiting' replicates the sound of a car's engine ticking over. The sound is persistent, increasing the tension.

Page 29 Margin 1
Readers are familiar with the shocking effect of a poltergeist in a room. Here the improbable acts shock in a humorous fashion.

Page 31 Margin 1
The irregular rhythm reflects the man's unhappiness in this urban environment. He has lost the even rhythm of the music of his island home.

Practice 2
'sun surfacing' – the repetition of the sibilant represents the smooth movement of the sun rising above the waves.

'groggily groggily' – represents the slow, jerky movement of his mind back to consciousness. The sound reflects the lurching movement of a drunk.

'muffling muffling' – an onomatopoeic representation of unclear sounds.

Page 32 Margin 1
Prejudiced people see only half the story. They choose what they see to be the wrong half of somebody, say his or her appearance, and judge the whole person accordingly.

(Teenagers with the 'wrong' hairstyle must be hooligans.)

Page 33 Margin 1
A meal between two people who love each other can take on the feeling of a spiritual meeting.

Practice 1
The repetition of 'half' emphasises the fact that prejudiced people only see half of everything. They then form a judgement of the whole. From an imperfect viewing of a painting, the weather, a part-realised dream, everything being viewed with only half an eye, judgements are made. Prejudiced people assume things, wrongly, from a limited standpoint.

Page 34 Margin 1
The people had become desensitised by war. Where they were full of life they have now lost all feeling.

Margin 2
The natural steady tread of the water buffalo symbolised the confidence the people had in their way of life.

Page 35 Margin 1
A squatter takes over a house and lives there illegally. The development has taken over the natural environment although it should not be there.

Practice 1
lanterns – household objects would indicate their domestic life; decorative things would show their artistic ability.

ceremonies – reveal social duties and what the people held sacred.

ornaments – reveal personal taste and values.

epic poem – stories about types of people and actions which their society valued.

Page 36 Margin 1
The room is searching for complete freedom. A place with empty air would provide that.

Margin 2
Possible meanings:
The events are so interesting that nobody wants to leave.
Nobody feels threatened by these improbable events.

Page 37 Margin 1
She is so used to hurricanes that another one makes her feel that life is going on normally.

Margin 2
The hurricane acts like a fuse blowing at home when the house is plunged into darkness. In this instance it short-circuits her thoughts and feelings.

Practice 2
dark ancestral spectre – the storm reminds her of a threatening ghost of one of her ancestors.

old tongues – the winds sound like ancient languages, whose meaning has been lost.

blinding illumination – the lightning reveals everything in a flash, so powerful that you are momentarily blinded.

crusted roots – the roots are so old that they have grown hard coverings.

the frozen lake – the speaker has lost the ability to feel, as though she is a mass of solid ice.

Page 38 Margin 1
Seeing the vultures in human terms make them appealing to the reader. The poet's humorous treatment of them enables the reader to overlook some of their more disgusting habits.

Margin 2
'perpetuity' means that this man's evil goes on for ever. There is no let-up.

Page 39 Margin 1
They have nothing to be happy about, nothing of their way of life left to celebrate.

Page 43 Margin 1
The costumes represent a people who are intensely proud of their culture and wish to show it off.

Page 44
The man is only interested in immediate pleasure, tasting a yam. More serious issues do not concern him.

Page 49 Margin 1
e.g. build and run animal shelters; give first aid and essential medication to a rescued animal; return injured or orphaned animals to their natural habitat; give veterinary care to beaten or tortured animals.

Page 50 Margin 1
sorry; disgraceful

Page 51 Margin 1
First is a fact.

Practice
Facts: e.g. alarms set off the car's horn or their own sounder; a siren is a distinctive sound; many alarms knock out the car's ignition; many alarms go off only for a limited time.

Opinions: e.g. a cut-off could be bad if it left the car exposed; a car alarm that goes off unnecessarily... can drive people nearby to distraction; using the car's horn might be a bit of a risk; flashing headlights are likely to raise eyebrows.

Page 52 Margin 1
e.g. I couldn't cope at home; all the guilt and social pressures are horrendous; people are shocked, I was scared she'd need nursing care; I was worried that Mum would be put in a room full of mad people.

Page 53 Margin 1
First sentence, second para.

Practice
1) Pace of change is difficult for older people; it is too fast.
2) Uses a well known saying; says that older people have to accept it.
3) She does not accept the fact that older people have to accept change; she would rather we looked backwards.
4) He makes a change in the status of the monarchy, itself an important issue.
5) She is prepared to have a go with new technology.
6) Those of Age Concern. It identifies with the Queen and repeats her central idea.

Page 55 Margin 1
Designed for people seeking information on Brit Awards; full explanations on a range of FAQ's.

Page 56 Margin 1
Uses smoke, the object of the message; shaped like an open mouth gasping for breath.

Page 57 James Villas
1) Emphasises hospitality.
2) Customises site for each individual's needs.
3) Gives impression of range of accommodation.
4) Allows them an impression of where they might go; adds to honesty of firm in showing off their accommodation.

Oxfam
1) As many as 5.
2) Emboldens and italicises key features.
3) Visual presentation of effect of small donation.
4) Emphasises contentment and happy lifestyle.

Page 59 Margin 2
e.g. Hands up; down the loo; spud; hand on their heart.

Practice
1) Large; predatory; evasive.
2) e.g. peril; decimate.
3) e.g. exotic; gobble up; devastated; wily; causing havoc. All give an impression of something big, alien and savage.

Page 60 Margin 1
Text A is about the attractions of North Cyprus.
Text B tells the reader about the writer's memories of Cyprus,.

Margin 2
Text A: attract holiday visitors – persuade
Text B: entertain/inform.

Page 65 Practice
Intrested = interested; cylcling = cycling; weels = wheels; bmx = BMX followed by full stop; where = wear.

Page 68 Margin 2
Verbs: Is, has. Is kept, has, are looked after, has, is, swim, have, will allow, to play, will give, are, want, stay up.
Adjectives: nice, long, clean, busy, local, smashing, yellow, local, temporary, young.

Page 70 Margin 1
7 imperatives. Bullet points.

Margin 2
1000 children under the age of 15; pedestrians killed in road accidents; 57,800 people found guilty or cautioned for drunkenness.

Margin 3
Positive, friendly tone – like a conversation with a friend.

Page 71 Margin 1
e.g. awareness of size of school; awareness of support available; awareness of change in variety of curriculum.

Page 73 Box B
1) Case in Court of Human Rights
2) Control of children by parents.
3) 2nd and 3rd sections.
4) Use of sub headings and sub sections to break up the text.

Page 75 Margin 1
Direct quotes and summaries of opinions; indication of tone of speaker, e.g. 'rhapsodically'.

Page 76 Margin 1
e.g. runs deep; slipped twinkling; strong and rocky; mottled, white, recumbent limbs; arch.

Page 78 Margin 1
At the end of a sentence giving an instruction; to express an extreme reaction, e.g. 'Oh no!'

Page 79 Margin 1
It is a report, therefore the events must have already occurred.